By Order of

Napoleon

THE TAKING OF MALTA

By Order of
Napoleon

THE TAKING OF MALTA

Napoleon's Orders
Compiled and Translated
by Joe Scicluna

Revised 3rd Edition

ISBN-13: 978-1986977906
ISBN-10: 1986977900

License Note

CONTENTS

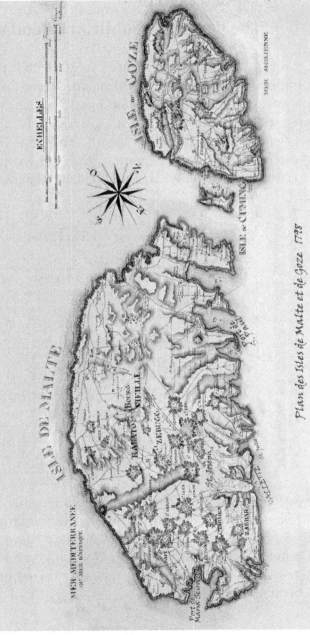

ISLE DE MALTE

MER MEDITERRANÉE
OU MER D'AFRIQUE

ÉCHELLES

ISLE DU GOZE

ISLE DU CUMINO

MER SICILIENNE

Plan des Isles de Malte et de Goze 1798

The French Republican Calendar

From 1792 to 1806, France adopted the French republican calendar and also introduced a new system of measurements, the metric system, which is still used today in most countries. The French calendar was not as successful. The new French calendar had twelve months, each of which had exactly 30 days which were divided into three *decades*.

The New Republican Calendar

New Name	Meaning	Time Period
Vendemaire	Vintage	September 22 – October 21
Brumaire	Fog	October 22 – November 20
Frimaire	Frost	November 21 – December 20
Nivose	Snow	December 21 – January 19
Pluviose	Rain	January 20 – February 18
Ventose	Wind	February 19 – March 20
Germinal	Budding	March 21 – April 19
Floreal	Flowers	April 20 – May 19
Prairial	Meadow	May 20 – June 18
Messidor	Harvest	June 19 – July 18
Thermidor	Heat	July 19 – August 17
Fructidor	Fruit	August 18 – September 21

At the end of the year, following 30 Fructidor, were five special "complementary" days to round out the year to 365 days. The complementary days were named Virtue, Genius, Labor, Opinion and Rewards. Year 1 of the revolutionary calendar corresponds to September 1792.

Preface

Napoleon issued thousands of dispatches directives and orders during the many campaigns of his military career. This e-book is a chronological compilation of his orders concerning the taking of Malta in 1798. They include orders to capture Gozo, Mdina and of course the city of Valletta. Napoleon's orders were very specific in terms of how the French were to treat the Knights, the Maltese, and the clergy. They included radical health and education reforms intended to align Malta's administration to the new revolutionary ideology of the French republic. He abolished nobility and slavery. He reorganized the clergy and redefined its sphere of influence. He also ordered the removal of the Order's silver and precious stones from St. John's Cathedral in Valletta.

The goal is not to judge, praise or criticize the French occupation of Malta, but to give the reader access to source documents and hopefully give some perspective to those momentous events that radically changed the course of Malta's history.

By Order of

Napoleon

The Taking of Malta

Napoleon Bonaparte

The Poussielgue Report

As Napoleon was preparing his expedition to take possession of Malta on his way to Egypt, he sent an envoy on a secret mission to the island. He wanted to assess to what extent he could count on the support of the Maltese population and the Order's French knights. Jean-Baptiste Poussielgue, whose cousin resided at Malta as Captain of the Port, was assigned this reconnaissance mission. He visited Malta six months before the French fleet sailed into the ports of Malta. This is the report Poussielgue submitted to Napoleon, as published by Clément de La Jonquière in his book *L'expédition d'Égypte, 1798-1801.*

Jean Baptiste Poussielgue

Milan, Le 20 Pluviose Year VI
(February 8th, 1798)

Citizen General,

I arrived in Malta on December 24th, the eve of Christmas festivities. The Grand Master was reinstating the old traditional ceremonies that had long been forgotten and abandoned by his predecessors. Throughout my 18-day visit, I was able to witness all of these ceremonies. The knights themselves had no recollection of such pathetic pageantry, as they looked on in disbelief.

Currently the Order has about six hundred knights in Malta. Two-thirds of them are French. Generally speaking the French represent half of the Order's members, and most of them are based in Malta. The new Grand Master, Hompesch, owes his election to the French knights. During his election campaign, he promised them he would continue giving them the same support they had received from his predecessor, De Rohan. Before being elected Grand Master, he was the Emperor's[1] minister at Malta and as such, he was a staunch defender of Austria's interests.

No sooner was he elected than he declared he was no longer the Emperor's minister, that all nations would be treated equally and that he would continue in his endeavours to preserve the Order's independence and prosperity. He seized the

---

[1] Paul I of Russia

opportunity to show his goodwill towards the French even before we made peace with the Emperor. He refused to associate the Order with the proposals made by certain French knights against the French Republic and its government.

The Grand Master is a very popular man and is also very generous. He likes to be seen in public and often throws money at the gathering crowds. He is extremely polite and affable with everybody. Although his knowledge is very limited, he has good judgment and managed to earn himself the respect and affection of the knights of all the *Langues*. He is just as liked and respected by the Maltese population. To his credit one might also add that he is very discreet and not one to share his inner secrets. Until now, I have not met anyone who can be considered his exclusive confidant or having any significant influencing power on his decisions.

Ultimately, I can say that throughout my stay on Malta I heard only good things about him, from the Maltese, from French and foreign knights, from the aristocrats and also from the democrats. I was able to witness the devotion of the people who come from all corners of the island to gather around the palace just for the pleasure of catching a glimpse of him. Given the circumstances[1], he has shown a remarkable political ability that has earned him

---

[1] The Order was facing financial ruin and its relations with France became strained after the French Government expropriated all the Order's properties in France.

unprecedented popularity.

The Grand Master has the full allegiance of the Order's Council, even though it only carries two votes. Nevertheless, he has the exclusive right to grant any kind of privilege or employment and this makes him one of the most absolute Princes in Europe, particularly since the *Langues* of France are now totally under the Order's control.

Among the three or four hundred French knights based on Malta only fifteen or twenty of them are in favour of the French Republic and its government. The rest of them are all staunch royalists and they will never change. They spend most of their time criticising the Directory and the Councils and even the Republican Army. Nevertheless many patriotic knights believe they secretly regret having committed themselves to the opposite party and would gladly switch sides were it not for the false sense of shame from adhering to new principles that the Order had always fought against.

The knights' livelihood is totally dependent on the Order and in return they are totally devoted to defending its interests, for if the Order ceased to exist, they would be left without any means or resources. The Grand Master fully understands this and he relies entirely on them to defend the palace if it were to be attacked. The knights of the other countries do not carry much weight in Malta, for most of them do not reside here. They tend to be somewhat indifferent towards the French

Revolution.

The more affluent Maltese and the seamen secretly despise the Order. The former because they are totally excluded from all government decisions, since the Maltese are not allowed to become Knights of Malta and the latter because of the Order's policy of war against the Barbary States which are their primary enemy. The Order forbids Maltese ships from trading with them, which consequently exposes them to the risk of being captured and taken as slaves, a fate that is worse than death itself.

The Maltese bear the burden of despotism and aristocracy more than any other country. They are imprisoned if they are caught walking the streets without a light after certain hours. Only knights have the right to be 'without light'. The first ten or twelve rows of the theatre are always reserved exclusively for knights. No Maltese can occupy these seats even if they are all empty. The Maltese have to settle for the back rows having to mix with the lackeys. The aristocracy also exerts its authority very heavily with society in general and particularly in the courts of criminal and civil affairs. The Grand Master enjoys excessive rights and can even suspend the course of justice if, for any reason, the court's decisions do not suit him.

Malta has its own nobility. The Grand Master often grants titles of nobility to obtain money and to obtain the support of the principal families. These nobles however are not given any particular rights or privileges over other Maltese and they continue to be barred from the Order of Malta. Consequently, the Maltese nobility bears more animosity for it hurts their pride to hold distinguishing titles without enjoying any of the associated privileges.

On arriving at Malta, I sensed a general concern about the intentions of the French Republic. Journals from Paris and Milan have reported that France was planning to take Malta. Two French frigates had just moored at their port for a few days. That in itself, coupled with my unexpected presence, was enough to cause alarm in this little country that ever since the war considers itself as prey to the whole of Europe.

I visited the Grand Master the day after my arrival. I also met with various bailiffs, commanders and knights to whom I was recommended with letters of credentials. The Grand Master treated me very politely but was very reserved. The others seemed more intrigued than anything else. I also met many members of the Order at the home of my cousin, the captain of the Port of Malta. His home is a place of social gatherings where the patriots meet in the morning and the aristocrats meet in the evening. All of them want to return to France and, except for twelve or fifteen patriots and a few moderate aristocrats, none of them are likely to ever overcome the hate and revulsion they have against the Republic. It will not be a simple task to try to sway these people through favours.

I wasted no time in testing the waters and fulfilling the objective of my mission. I referred to a number of people whom I recognised as being the more intellectual and the more fervent patriots. They all welcomed me with enthusiasm. We had open discussions during ten or twelve different sessions in which we explored the best means of uniting Malta to France as rapidly and as smoothly as possible. The conclusion from these discussions was that we must waste no time in carrying out some plan of integration otherwise Malta could fall into the hands of another power.

The Grand Master, the knights, and the Maltese are all perfectly aware that the Order is badly lacking in funds without which it could soon cease to exist. Under such circumstances, I would not be surprised if the Grand Master was holding secret negotiations to relinquish Malta to England, or Russia, or to the King of Naples, while he was still in a position to negotiate.

The knights and the population of Malta are generally antagonistic towards the English. They hope we will be able to temporarily counter them if they attempted to take Malta without the Grand Master's consent. The English have already made attempts at negotiating. They sent a certain Chevalier De Sade who made an open proposal to the Grand Master and to the Order's high-ranking officers. His proposal fell on deaf ears and he left empty-handed.

We need not be too concerned about Russia given the geographic distance between the two countries. Our biggest concern lies with the Emperor firstly because by taking possession of Malta he would significantly enhance the value of his territories in the Adriatic which today are undermined by the neighbouring islands that are under our control and secondly because the Emperor has more means than any other country to compensate the Grand Master, who is German. He has the means to negotiate the Grand Master's resignation to his advantage. A resignation that is bound to happen sooner or later.

The Maltese are more inclined to favour the French more than any other nation. Nevertheless, we cannot expect them to help us or fight for our cause. The best we can hope for is that they would not take up arms against us if France were to attack Malta.

It is impossible to infiltrate the knights, or the population, in the hope of creating a dissident group in favour of France. The Order is extremely vigilant to the extent that nobody would be willing to take such a risk. Besides, the Grand Master has been so successful at winning over the public that he would be immediately informed of any plot that may be hatched against him. Despite its limited force, the Order remains on permanent guard and cannot be taken by surprise. They are perfectly capable of resisting an open attack until another nation comes to their aid.

If we were to launch a surprise attack, or an open attack, and failed, we would be totally shamed in the eyes of Europe and would be subjected to the same resentment that all nations have towards England. Such consequences are inevitable when the Law of Nations is breached without the backing of a successful outcome.

It would probably be easier to win Malta over through negotiations rather than force, or better still to employ both simultaneously. To succeed with negotiations we would first have to make it clear to the Grand Master that he has no hope of preserving the Order. We can easily achieve this by engaging the Court of Spain and have them confiscate the Order's properties in their country. These properties can be used as collateral payment to supplement the treasury of this court. If Spain were to have strong reservations about carrying out such a scheme, we can easily overcome this. We can force the Pope to suppress the Order with one stroke of the pen. The suppression would be welcomed by the sovereigns of all nations as all of them covet the properties of the Order of Malta.

While we show willingness to negotiate with Rome and Spain, the executive Directory of France would send a Plenipotentiary Minister to take up residence at Malta and hold secret negotiations with the Grand Master for the handover of Malta. In exchange we could either offer him another island over which he can exercise sovereign rights for the rest of his life, or we could offer him a sum of money. We can also choose to offer both. The Grand Master considers it important to be perceived as the sovereign. He is also lacking funds due to the huge debts he has accumulated over the years.

It should not be too difficult to bring the Grand Master to the negotiating table; we would first have to convince him that the suppression of the Order and the loss of all his revenues are inevitable. Secondly, we would demonstrate how no other nation could guarantee the same level of compensation as France and that even if England made wonderful offers, it would not honour any of its commitments as soon as Malta fell into its hands. Russia, on the other hand, can only offer money. Given its state of affairs with Germany, it is in no position to offer any sovereign state in exchange for Malta.

I have explored different means for taking Malta, through surprise or through force. The element of surprise is possible only if we had our own men within the city. However, it would be impossible to have them deployed at all the necessary points or even at one single point. Even the most avid patriots are against deploying such means. The knights have courage but their strong principles of honour stop them from adopting what they call means of *betrayal*. Besides, as I mentioned earlier there are only about fifteen patriots who can influence and only three or four of them have real determination. They are however willing to explore if it is at all feasible to employ the means of a surprise attack.

Many options could be used separately or simultaneously. The first would be to take control of

19

the city's portside entrance, during the night. This would require us to have two ships and two frigates moored inside the harbour with 1,500 soldiers on board. The gate is normally guarded by only fifteen or twenty soldiers. They may take extra precautions and increase the guard to thirty or forty men when they see the French ships entering the harbour. We would have to be very cautious for the first five or six days. It would be quite easy for ten or twelve of our men to take them by surprise, take control of the gate, and make sure it is kept open until further troops disembarked from our ships. Admittedly, it is a risky operation. If we fail to take control of the gate, the ships at the harbour would be immediately blasted by the numerous batteries of Fort St Angelo whose cannons are always ready to fire. However, if we succeed in taking control of the port we also have control over the city and if we control the city we control the island.

Inside the city they have granaries where their grain is stored. There is also a powder store, an arsenal and their treasury. The Grand Master and almost all of the knights reside within the city. Once we have taken control of the city we can make generous offers to the Maltese and to the knights, even to those who had taken up arms. It is very likely they will give themselves up. Either way, the 1,500 men would need the backing of a company that would be moored at the port of Marsa-Muciet[1].

---

[1] Marsamxett harbour

The men could easily take Fort St Elmo and all the fortifications to the west of the city.

The second option would be to scale the ramparts situated between Fort St Elmo and the area reserved for communicating with ships before they go into quarantine. This operation seems to be a safer option in that it would be carried out during the night, hence our ships would be less exposed. In addition, since all warships are bound to go into quarantine before entering the port, it would be very difficult to carry out the first option and take the gate by surprise. On the other hand, with the second option the ships can be moored close to the ramparts as they are being climbed. It should not be too difficult to overcome the two or three guards at the Health Office. The ramparts in this area are no more than twelve to fifteen feet high due to the rubble piled up at the bottom all the way down to the sea. Our ships will be ready and equipped with ladders and other tools. The first thirty men to reach the top of the ramparts will protect the remaining troops as they make their way up.

Another alternative (this one is for those experts who believe it would be too difficult to take control of the city and that even if we did, it would serve no purpose) would be a simultaneous attack on Fort Ricazoli and Fort St Elmo. We would also disembark four or five thousand men at the port of Marsa-Sirocco who would first take Villa Cottonera and subsequently attack Fort Ricazoli. If we succeed in taking this fort along with that of St Elmo, Malta will be under our control for they will have no means of bringing in reinforcements. This option however requires us to act openly. We may have to resort to such an option if the negotiations with the Grand Master fail.

The Order of Malta alone cannot defend itself for too long from an open attack. They are lacking equipment and above all, they are lacking men. We can be quite certain the Maltese will not fight to defend the Order. Their forces can be summed up as follows:

- 200 men stationed at Fort St Elmo make up the Grand Master's Guard. Thirty guards take up their post each day. The Grand Master's palace has 16, the Customs House has four and St Elmo has ten.
- 450 men compose the Malta Regiment. 42 of them guard the entrances and 24 are in reserve. This regiment also provides guard service for the prisons, the quarter and a few other posts. One of its companies is stationed at Fort St Angelo.
- 300 men form the Galley Corps. Twenty of them guard the palace of the General of the Galleys.
- 300 galley soldiers. All of them are stationed on the island or city of Vittoriosa.
- 80 men at Fort Ricazoli
- 80 men at Fort Manoel

- 800 infantry. These are brought into service only on special occasions. They wear uniforms but are paid only if they render services. They are based in the countryside.

All this adds up to 2,210 men to which one must add the National Guard or the Militia, which is estimated at 10,000 men. They are not very skilled and are not assigned to any services. Among all these men there are hardly any officers and the few gunners are not very well trained.

Malta's principal force consists of the three to four hundred French knights. Only they can put up any significant resistance, because they are French and therefore they are brave but also because Malta is their only refuge and they will fight to the bitter end to keep it in their possession.

It is evident the Order has considerably more French knights than of any other nation. This is evident judging by the table allowances paid out in cash by the treasury to all the knights living on Malta. For the year starting in May 1, 1796 up to May 1, 1797 *(V.S.)*, a total of 18,267 ecus was paid of which 10,777 were for knights of the three French *Langues* and only 7,489 was paid for all the other remaining *Langues*[1].

Malta has enough grain provisions to last eight months. As of January 1, 1798 *(V.S,)* they had 31,468

---

[1] This level of detail was very likely provided by Bosredon de Ransijat, a French knight who at the time was the Order's treasurer

salmes of grain, equivalent to about 80,000 quintals. The consumption for December 1797 was 3,946 *salmes*. At the time of my departure there was a severe shortage of wood and they had no means of bringing in any imports due to Barbary corsairs. The public bakeries had to use rotten wood recovered from old boat wrecks to light their furnaces. There is no shortage of powder or water but they do lack artillery and good calibre shot.

All the patriots I spoke with at Malta believe that if we were to take Malta through force or through negotiation, we must first overcome one major obstacle, that is, the French knights. There is no point in trying to win them over with promises of a safe return to France. They will not give up Malta, especially if they are not given any guarantee for their future. They believe the simplest and possibly the most practical course would be to have them all repatriated by way of a decree stating clearly that the Order's claims for compensation for their expropriated properties will be refused. Since the Knights of Malta had become members of an Order that was considered a foreign power before the Revolution, according to the Constitution they ceased to be French. The decree can therefore state that they would not be considered as *émigrés*[1] but merely as foreigners. Under such conditions they will be able to return to France and take full

---

[1] Émigrés were considered enemies of the Republic and therefore not allowed to re-enter France.

possession of their properties.

If it is not possible for the Directory to issue such a special decree I believe it should be possible to apply some form of an existing law instead. It may not have the same impact but it should be enough to make them promptly pack their bags given their naivety and their eagerness to return to France.

If the Directory chose to negotiate with the Grand Master this could be an important concession to put forward as every knight would then have a stake in the success of these negotiations. This would put added pressure on the Grand Master to accept the terms being offered.

During my stay at Malta I made promises and sowed the seeds of hope albeit without taking unnecessary risks of being exposed. I made no secret of the fact that the Executive Directory was concerned about the intentions of Russia and England and that despite their *émigrés* status, the French Knights of Malta had not yet been totally excluded from France. The two Councils and the Directory have yet to decide on their final status and if they want a positive outcome and a prompt return to France they must give service and demonstrate their loyalty to the new government. I advised them it is their duty to make sure that the English are not allowed to take control of such an important island, regardless of their personal opinions. They are the enemy of France and of all French people. If Malta is destined to lose its independence then it is the duty of the French knights to pave the way and unite the island with France rather than allowing any other power to take control. I instructed my two or three 'apostles', to whom I have confided the secret of my mission, to spread this doctrine. The word has already reached several aristocrats and they continue to spread the message.

I am convinced my endeavours would have brought swift results were it not for the report prepared by Deputy Laloi for the Council which was followed by a decree refuting the compensation claims made by the Knights of Malta. The fact that the news of the decree reached Malta while I was out there certainly had a dampening effect on my wonderful promises.

Malta is so well fortified they are able to resist attack for a considerable time with few men or resources. However, there is much truth in the belief that the fortress is more than half conquered if we first succeed in getting rid of the four hundred French knights. This is the opinion of all the different types of patriots I met at Malta. They had diverging opinions on everything else but on this point they were unanimous. They believe it would be quicker, easier and safer to take them out of Malta rather than trying to bait them with promises, for when they are united as a body, it is impossible to sway them even though individually their desires are very much aligned with our objectives.

A few days before my departure from Malta there were rumours that a fleet of forty English vessels had entered the Mediterranean intending to take possession of Minorca and Majorca. The Grand Master held a secret council session and spent several hours behind closed doors with his Chief of Artillery. Apparently, he gave orders to immediately place the island in a state of alert to defend from an English attack. However, a group of patriots, and myself, believe this was just a ruse, that he was discreetly preparing their defence against us rather than the English. As a matter of fact one patriot who was in daily contact with the Grand Master told me that his latest suspicion was that the two French frigates that had entered the harbour before my arrival and left the day before my departure, were there to assess the situation and sow the seeds of revolt. The Grand Master believes I was there on a similar mission and that I was chosen because of my success during the revolution of Genoa. Finally he also believes the French squadron at Corfu is only waiting for my signal to start heading for Malta and take over the island. I did not express any more concern towards this rumour than I did for the thousands of others caused by his agitation and worry. I was simply amused by the fact that the English, for whom he is allegedly preparing his defence, are none other than ourselves.

I am convinced that if the English attacked Malta they will be met with the strongest resistance. There are only two or three Bailiffs within the council that ever dared speak favourably of the English. No knight from other nations has ever supported them and the French knights are fervently opposed.

It is inconceivable for a Frenchman not to want to see Malta fall into French hands. We have had very little opportunity so far to appreciate the advantages it has to offer because we have always been able to reap its benefits since France has always had a majority representation within the Order. As such, we have always considered Malta as being French. However if Malta were to fall under into the hands of another power, such as the English, or the Emperor, then we will certainly begin to realise its full value.

First and foremost, Malta is the key to the Levant. Very few ships will make the voyage to the Levant without having to stop at Malta. Since we controlled practically all the commerce in the Levant, none of the other nations valued Malta as much as France did. The loss of Malta would be less felt by the other nations for this very reason. Whereas for us, losing Malta would mean the end of our commerce and would render our conquests in the Levant worthless, for the value of these conquests depends on the free communication between them.

Politically speaking, he who controls Malta controls commerce in the Mediterranean. This island has the safest and the most beautiful ports that have ever existed. They are vast, plentiful and suitable for all winds. Its fortifications make it impregnable even in the hands of a second-rate power. It is another

Gibraltar. Without any hesitation, I can say that these benefits, and many others which I will not dwell on, would give us the greatest advantage that France could ever hope for from this war. We must therefore not hesitate in applying all the means we have available to acquire the island, even if we have to make financial sacrifices towards the Grand Master and the knights. We must do whatever it takes for we will reap the rewards within Malta itself.

At this point Poussielgue gave a very detailed account of the Order's assets and financial resources including those of Malta's churches. He also outlined the Order's revenues prior to the Revolution in which he reported a surplus of 128,246 livres.

[Clément de La Jonquière]

Since the Revolution, however, the Order has lost all its revenues from France and most of its revenues from Germany and Italy. It also has to provide subsidies for the French knights who no longer received pensions from their Commanderies. The net result is a deficit estimated at about two million livres. The Order cannot possibly sustain such as state of affairs for very long. It can make use of a few external resources to hold out for one more year but ultimately it will collapse under its own weight. Their fate is only too evident for both the Maltese as well as all the knights.

Poussielgue goes on to mention the Università which functioned like a bank and administered the buying and selling of grain. On January 1ˢᵗ, 1798 its treasury reported a deficit of more than four million livres. The situation was alarming in that the livelihood of the entire population depended on the provisioning of grain. He gave further details on Malta's industry and agriculture and concluded his report as follows:

[Clément de La Jonquière]

Malta cannot hold out much longer and the Grand Master knows this. It will inevitably fall into the hands of another power. We need to be even more wary about the Emperor rather than the English. Having possessed Venice, he will also want to have his own naval force, for commercial purposes if nothing else. He will certainly have his eyes set on Malta to help him achieve this objective. The fact that we retained the Venetian isles means we hold the key to the Adriatic but if he were to take possession of Malta, which is the key to the Mediterranean, he stands to gain significantly more than he has lost and we would lose significantly more than we have gained. The Emperor's strong ties with the Court of Naples could facilitate his task, which is perfectly aligned with Austria's expansionist ambitions, given that the Queen of Naples protects Austria.

I spoke earlier of possible negotiations with the Grand Master. Here is another alternative, which could be more appropriate, given that it would be less costly. It involves taking advantage of the situation in Rome to open simultaneous negotiations with Naples and with the Grand Master. We could negotiate some form of compensation to Naples for giving up its sovereignty and offer compensation to the Grand Master for giving up Malta. The King of Naples wants Benevento, which is enclaved within his estate. Not only could we give it to him, we could also give him other parts of the Pope's estates as long as he willing to hand over Malta's sovereign rights to France and give the Grand Master lifetime sovereignty over a principality in Sicily and over other properties in Elba that are owned by the King. In addition, France could grant him one million *livres*, which would first be used to settle his debts. It would be best to mention this sum in the formal agreement to guarantee and seal our acquisition.

If we were to adopt the idea of negotiating with the Grand Master we will need to send over someone he trusts, a good mediator with a firm but conservative character. He will need to be given credibility with titles like Special Envoy, or Plenipotentiary Minister, to inspire trust and respect. This agent will be responsible for the negotiations and for making sure the Maltese become accustomed to seeing French ships in their ports. He will need to be able to communicate with the squadron at Corfu so that at his first signal they would head straight for Malta and take possession of the island either through force or through peaceful means.

If we succeed in convincing the Spanish to

expropriate the Order's properties, it would give us a considerable advantage since it would eliminate the Order's last resource and place the Grand Master at our mercy. Whichever way we take Malta, our success depends on being able to expel all the French knights by allowing them to return to France.

Citizen Picot has a very good reputation at Malta. He is respected by the patriots and by everyone else. The Executive Directory could make good use of him in our expedition. It would be worthwhile to consider his immediate assignment to the squadron at Corfu and promote him to the rank of Combat Engineer.

Should you require any further details, Citizen General, I hope to join you very shortly where I will be able to brief you in person.

Greetings and Respect, Poussielgue

The Taking of Malta

Directive
Paris, 23 Germinal Year VI
(12th April, 1798)

From the Executive Directory

The Order of Malta has deliberately taken a hostile stance against France since the beginning of the current war. This was officially stated by the Grand Master[1] in a declaration he made on October 10, 1794. In his insolent act he stated that he had neither the desire nor the intention to recognize the French republic. He constantly emphasized this sentiment by giving his full support to the kings' coalition armies that fought against liberty. His acts against the republic reached a pinnacle just recently when he welcomed into his Order some of France's worst enemies who had taken up arms against the motherland. It is clear that the Grand Master has an imminent intention to surrender his territory to one of the powers that are still at war with France which would paralyse our navigation in the Mediterranean. The Order's stance towards the French republic is undeniably the same as that of other enemy powers. The nation considers itself in a state of war brought about by the Order itself

---

[1] Emmanuel de Rohan-Polduc (1725-1797)

without making any formal declaration. The executive directory therefore does not require authorisation from any legal body to justify the measurers taken against the Order to defend its honour and national interest.

Orders are as follows:

Article 1.
The general-in-chief of the Army of the East is tasked with the mission to take possession of the Island of Malta.

Article 2.
To achieve this he will immediately assemble the naval and infantry forces under his command and head for the Island of Malta. This directive must not be printed.

Directive
Paris, 23 Germinal Year VI
(12th April, 1798)

From the Executive Directory

Article 1.
The order given today in a directive to General Bonaparte, commander of the Army of the East, will be carried out at a time based on his own judgment

such that it will not compromise the success of other missions of which he is in charge. The executive Directory insists that he exercises caution with regards to abovementioned point.

Article 2.
This directive must not be printed

To General Desaix
Paris, 30 Germinal Year VI
(19th April, 1798)[I]

I have received no news since the 15th. I am departing tomorrow for Toulon. The fleet will set sail and head straight for Saint-Pierre on *Floreal* 10.The convoy of Genoa will depart on the 7th to the seas of Toulon. You will shortly receive orders to depart on the 15th. You will sail along the coast of Naples and past the lighthouse of Messina. You will moor at Syracuse or at any other convenient spot in the vicinity with easy access to Malta. You will need one frigate, two brigs, two dispatch boats and two transport galleys. You are advised to acquire two more good dispatch boats, either by taking two French Corsairs and deploying officers and good men on board, or by finding two good sail boats locally. Our meeting point will be Malta.

[I] The original letter signed by Napoleon is displayed at the Malta Maritime Museum

République   Française

Liberté   Égalité

Au Quartier Général de Paris le 30 germinal an 6e de la République
Une et Indivisible

Bonaparte Général en Chef

Au général Desaix.

Je n'ai point de vos nouvelles depuis le 8. Je pars demain pour toulon. les ordre mettre à la voile le 10 floréal et se dirigera droit sur la isle St pierre. le convoi qui en à gênes part le 9 pour se rendre dans la rade de toulon.

Vous aurez des ordre suffisamment pour partir le 8, côtoyer toutes les côtes de naples, passer le phare de messine et mouiller a Syracuse ou dans toute autre rade a au les environ plus favorable pour se rendre maître.

Vous devez avoir une frégatte, 2 Xbeck, 2 avisos et deux galéres du pape. et feroit à dessein que vous puissiez vous procurer deux autre avisos bon voilier, soit en arrêtant deux corsaire français et mettrant de

36

officiers et des marins intelligents à bord, fait et ...
... de deux bons voiliers du pays.

Notre point de réunion sera fixe Malthe.

Quoique nous n'ayons aucun ... quelques anglais ...
en voulant passer le détroit, cependant la ...
... par vos aventures me fait préférer de vous faire
filer côte à côte. il sera cependant nécessaire que vous
expédiez un aviso aux isles ft. pierre pour croiser
entre la Sardaigne et l'Afrique afin que s'il y avoit
des anglais arrivant aux isles ft. pierre avant nous
vous puissiez en être prévenu et régler vos mouvements
en conséquence.

... que vous soyez dans un port d'aventures
soit dans un de ces ... Vous n'avez rien à

craindre des anglais mais la première vent que vous
pourrez ... vous feriez, donc embarquez —

    1. pierre de ...
    2. mortiers
    2. grilles à boulet rouge.
    2 ou 300 coups par pierre.
afin de pouvoir établir une bonne batterie ... d'ailleurs
de pierre qui arrive dans l'endroit principal ...

Vous devez organiser votre départ à ... cachée ... afin
que tous les hommes malades ou en même de ... que vous
commandez puissent se réunir et filer à ... et mesure.

Je vous enverrai dire à ... jours ... ou ... positif pour
votre départ. ce que je vous en dis ici c'est pour que vous
vous prépariez et que vous puissiez d'avance dans le ...
les renseignements qui vous seront nécessaires.

Vous embarquerez avec vous le commissaire ...
et tous les hommes qui pourront à longue ... du
port de ... ... dont vous puissiez avoir besoin
ou le ... de ...

                        je vous salue.
                        Bonaparte

Although we have no idea where the English fleet is or where it is heading, I prefer that you do not take any unnecessary risks and sail side by side. However, you will be required to send a dispatch boat to the Isles of Saint-Pierre[1] to patrol the seas between Sardinia and Africa. Should the English reach the isles of Saint Pierre before we do, we will be forewarned and we will take appropriate action.

Whether you are in a port on the continent or in a port in the two Sicilies, you need not to fear the English. Nevertheless, you must be prepared for them. You will therefore take on board four pieces of 24-calibre cannon, two mortars, and two grills to heat the round shot. You will form a good strong battery with two or three-hundred shot per piece.

You will assemble the troops under your command at Civita-Vecchia. I will send orders for your departure within four days. This directive is intended to give you the necessary time to prepare and to share with you the secret information that you need to know.

You will take on board with you Commissioner Menard and as many men as you need from Civita Vecchia. We will have them replaced from Toulon.

With my regards.

BONAPARTE

---

[1] Mediterranean islands, off Sardinia

François-Paul Brueys d'Aigalliers
(1753-1798)

To Admiral Brueys
On board *l'Orient*, 18 Prairial Year VI
(6th June, 1798)

Admiral Citizen, the general-in-chief has made his decisions concerning Malta and has ordered me to share them with you such that you can give the appropriate orders to the naval forces under your command.

The general-in-chief's plan is to have the squadron and the convoy occupy the bay of Marsa-Scirocco[l] as quickly as possible and to land the troops chosen for the Malta operation. Meanwhile, the second squadron consisting of the *le Franklin, le*

---

[l] Marsaxlokk in Southern Malta

Spartiale, l'Aquilon and *le Guerrier,* will take up positions at the entrance to the main port to block Malta's harbour.

The general-in-chief has appointed Commodore Decrès, captain of *la Diane,* to oversee the landing operations and hence ensure the general's protection.

The general-in-chief has designated the 4th and 7th demi-brigades and the 6th, the 19th and 80th battalions for the landing, supported by artillery. The abovementioned troops and artillery will disembark from the convoy warships and transports.

The general-in-chief wants each warship or transport ship to be responsible for disembarking its own troops. With regards to *le Franklin, le Spartiale, l'Aquilon* and *le Guerrier* which are blocking the harbour, they will lower their rowboats which will also be used to transport the troops of *l'Orient, le Tonnant, le Peuple Souverain* and *l'Heureux.*

Since *l'Orient* will have a considerable number of men on board, you will give orders to make use of the squadron's light vessels, like dispatch boats, *tartanes[1],* and landing boats.

The above plan requires you to give orders on land and on sea. You must be prepared to give the following orders as early as possible tomorrow morning.

----

[1] Mediterranean light boat

1. On the 19th, every ship must load arms onto the big boats; an *obusier*[I] or a *carronade*[II] and a number of *pierriers*[III] with forty shot and ready to be lowered.

2. Assemble at the stern the officers and commanders of all the units and detachments on board each transport vessel and warship. You will order them to inspect the garrison and the army troops to make sure that their arms are in good condition. You will ensure that each soldier is ready to disembark equipped with sixty cartridges and six flints.

3. You will Order the Corsican transport ships to be identifiable with a visible distinguishing mark. They will assemble around a warship which you will designate and which will have the same distinguishing mark.

4. Warn these ships that on the firing of three cannon shots from the flagship followed by another three from the convoy commander, they will join the frigate, *la Diane*, which will give the signal with four cannon shot. The frigate must have its own signal which you will define yourself and make known to the other ships.

[I] Shell-gun cannon
[II] Short smooth-bore cast iron cannon
[III] Small rock-firing cannon

The second set of orders concern the landing and they will be given to you once we approach Marsa-Scirocco. **[By order of the general-in-chief]**

To Admiral Brueys
On board *l'Orient*, 21 Prairial Year VI
(9th June, 1798)

Citizen General, the general-in-chief has tasked me to inform you that he wants you give orders for *la Serieuse* to assemble all the convoy ships from Genoa to be prepared to make a landing, either at the bay of *Vielle-Salines*[I] known by the name of *Mellecha*[II], or at St. Paul's bay, whichever is more convenient. You will inform the captain of *la Serieuse* that the landing will not begin until the general-in-chief gives the order. You will advise him not to carry out any hostile acts until then. As soon as the troops have landed we will take care of obtaining water and provisions.

The general-in-chief wants you to place the captain of *la Serieuse* under the command of General Baraguey d'Hilliers during the landing operation. Be aware that General Baraguey d'Hilliers has been given orders to land only the troops necessary to take control of the forts and the batteries, to allow

---

[I] Old salt pans
[II] Mellieha Bay, N. Malta

our convoy to moor and bring water and provisions on board.

By order of the general-in-chief

Louis Baraguey d'Hilliers

To General Baraguey d'Hilliers
On board *l'Orient*, 21 Prairial Year VI
(9th June, 1798)

Citizen General, in accordance with the plan of the general-in-chief, you need to be prepared to make a landing, either at the bay of *Vielle-Salines* or *Mellecha*, or at St. Paul's bay, to the north of Malta. Admiral Brueys has given orders for the convoy of Genoa to join the frigate *la Serieuse*. You will examine all the possible landing points in the vicinity of these two bays.

When you receive the order to land you will approach with a number of ships, from your convoy, that require water. You will use rowboats to land your men at the designated point. As soon as they land you will bring the water on board.

The general-in-chief wants you to land only the necessary troops to take control of the batteries and the towers to allow you to moor your convoy.

You will ensure that your convoy is ready to depart on the first order and that those men who are not destined to remain on Malta are ready to re-embark. The general-in-chief is assuming that you will need three to four days to replenish the ships with water.

You will inform the general-in-chief as soon as you have landed your men. He will give you new orders either by sea or via the Island of Malta.

Whilst on the island, the general-in-chief does not want you to do anything other than to occupy the points that protect your moorings while you bring water on board. The general-in-chief forbids the landing of any horses.

By order of the general-in-chief

General Louis Desaix

To General Desaix
On board *l'Orient*, off Malta, 21 Prairial
Year VI (9th June, 1798)

The general-in-chief orders General Desaix to depart as soon as possible on one of the galleys to patrol the coast of Malta from the bay of St. Thomas to that of *Vied-e-Sciaat*[I]. You are informed that the admiral has given orders for your convoy to go to the port of Marsa-Scirocco.

The general-in-chief wants you to identify the most appropriate landing points around Marsa-Scirocco. He wants you to disembark 300 or 400 men tomorrow morning before daybreak at your chosen

---

[I] Zurrieq. Southern Malta

landing point. You will land your rowboats at a safe distance from any batteries. Meanwhile you will bring in three of four of your ships using water replenishment as pretext. This will ensure the success of your landing operation.

Navy-general Du Chayla will moor four of his warships at a distance of one league outside Marsa-Scirocco to support you with the landing. All the men of the 80th demi-brigade, the 7th, the 19th and the 4th, that are on board General Du Chayla's ships will land at another point and join forces with your troops.

Once you are in control of the batteries and the towers and have safely moored your ships, the general-in-chief wants you to march into the city. You will attempt to penetrate through one of the gates or scale the walls of Cottonera at a point that has no ditch. However, should the enemy put up a defence, the general-in-chief wants you to march further on and take control Fort Ricasoli and the Cottonera walls. You will communicate with the General Vaubois' division, to your left, which should land at St. Julian's bay to take control of the other side of the city.

You will make sure not to land more troops than necessary for this operation, and no cavalry. As soon as your ships are in port, you will give orders to bring on board water and straw for the ships with horses. We need to be prepared to depart within three days. You will arrange to make bread and have your troops fed in the villages of Zabbar,

Zeitun, Gudia, and Tarshen[1].

The general-in-chief orders you to prepare everything for the landing tonight but do not initiate any form of hostilities until you receive new orders. You will tell the local inhabitants that you have no intention of changing their religion or beliefs, that discipline will be assured and that their priests and nuns will receive total protection. In addition, the general-in-chief will make an official proclamation to the whole island.

By order of the general-in-chief

---

[1] Tarxien, Southern Malta

Louis Alexandre Berthier
(1753-1815)

To General Berthier
On board *l'Orient*, off Malta, 21 Prairial
Year VI (9th June, 1798)

Citizen General, you will give the order to Admiral Brueys to assemble the Marseilles convoy around the frigate *l'Alceste* to be ready to disembark at Ramla Bay. The landing will take place once I give the order. The commander of the convoy is advised not to initiate any hostilities until then.

Should the admiral believe that the port of Miggiaro[1] is more appropriate for mooring he may choose to bring in the convoy as soon as the port is

---

[1] Mgarr

occupied by French troops.

He will place the captain of *l'Alceste* under the command of General Reynier for the landing operation.

By order of the general-in-chief

To General Berthier
On board *l'Orient*, off Malta,
21 Prairial Year VI (9th June, 1798)

The general-in-chief will give orders for General Reynier to be ready to make a landing at Ramla Bay and take control of the whole island of Gozo. Admiral Brueys has given orders for the Marseilles convoy to join the frigate *l'Alceste*. He will be ordered to do a reconnaissance tour of northern coast of the island of Gozo as soon as possible, with particular interest to Aain Rihana[1], Ramla Bay and other creeks such that he can identify the best landing point. Until the time when General Reynier has landed, you are advised not to engage in any hostilities that may cause concern to the local inhabitants.

As soon as General Reynier receives the order to land, he will approach with a number of convoy ships and request water provisions. He will land his men at the designated point using rowboats. As

---

[1] Rihana Valley, Ghajn Rihana

soon as they land you will bring the water and on board as well as straw for the stables. He will land only the necessary troops to take control of the island. He will name a chief-of-brigade or a chief-of-battalion and thereafter a commander for the whole island. The gunner company of the 4th demi-brigade is destined to remain on the island.

General Reynier will set up a hospital with 100 beds for sick soldiers. His entire division will be self-sufficient using resources available on the island.

He will prepare a simple proclamation which will be translated into local language and scribed by local clerks. The proclamation will state that the French have no intention of changing the religion or beliefs of the population, that order and discipline will be assured and that their priests will receive full protection. He will show particular respect towards the priests and monks. He will have seals placed on the chests containing the belongings of the Knights of Malta. He will transfer all arms to one location. If any of the villages appear to be belligerent he will take hostages on board the frigate.

General Reynier will report to me on how the inhabitants react and on the general sentiment on the island. I will give him instructions on what form of administration he needs to adopt and what further operations he will need to launch. None of the troops of his division are to remain on the island, other than the 4th demi-brigade. He must be ready to depart within three to four days.

No horses will disembark. The generals and

aide-de-camps can easily seize horses from the first village they come across.

General Reynier will take care that his men are fed with fresh meet. He will seek General Fugière on board *le Causse* and place himself under his command.

BONAPARTE

To General Berthier
On board *l'Orient*, 21 Prairial Year VI
(9th June, 1798)
Nine o'clock in the evening

Following his decision to attack the island and the possessions of the Order of Malta, the general-in-chief orders you to carry out the orders and instructions that I have already passed on to you and whose execution were awaiting the present order.

By order of the general-in-chief

Jean-Louis Reynier (1771-1814)

To General Reynier
On board *l'Orient*, 21 Prairial Year VI
(9th June, 1798)

Following orders from the general-in-chief, Citizen General, I am giving instructions to the war commissioner, M. Duprat to cater for the needs of your division for five days during their stay on the island of Gozo. I have also asked for one month of horse provisions and to be able to make use of any existing resources that belong to the Maltese government. I have tasked the commissioner to keep you informed and I have also have the honour to ask you to support these instructions with the help of your armed forces if necessary.

By order of the general-in-chief

August de Marmont
(1774-1852)

Maréchal Jean Lannes
(1769-1809)

To General Reynier
Off Malta, 21 Prairial Year VI
(9th June, 1798)

Following the orders of the general-in-chief, General Vaubois is ordered to depart on the 22nd at two o'clock in the morning to make a landing at a designated point between Saint Julien and Madliena Bay.

The troops commanded by Chief-of-brigade Marmont will march 100 or 200 *toises* ahead of General Lannes' brigade. On reaching the coast, Citizen Marmont will land his men at an

---

[1] 1 tois = approx. 6 feet

appropriate point of his choice. He will take control of any batteries that may obstruct his division's landing. Citizen Marmont will subsequently take up position at *Spinola Garden*.

General Lannes will send more detachments to take control of the batteries that dominate Madliena Bay such as the tower of Saint-Marc.

On the arrival of the 19th battalion, and the 4th demi-brigade, which are on board the Ajaccio convoy, Citizen Marmont will advance to blockade the city of La Valette. He will take control of the *City of Pinto*[I] up to *Casal Novo*[II] where he will join forces to the left of General Desaix.

The general will block the port of *Marsa-Muceit* and the unfinished fort located on Point Dragut. The three companies from the 18th and from the 32nd will form the main guard and will be deployed at *Cazal Gargur*.

A mobile unit formed by the 6th battalion will be deployed at *Cazal Lia,* and from *Cazal Attard* up to *Cité Vielle*[III] to obtain the surrender of the local inhabitants. General Vaubois will make a proclamation to reassure the inhabitants that they can continue to practice their religion, that law and order will be maintained, and that all villages will be protected as long as they cooperate.

The division's commission will make the necessary arrangements to have bread baked and to

---

[I] Town of Qormi
[II] Town of Paola, Rahal il- Gdid
[III] Mdina

provide food for the troops in the village. Adjutant-General Boyer will be temporarily attached to General Vaubois and his division during the landing operation.

By order of the general-in-chief

Order
On board *l'Orient*, off Malta, 21 Prairial
Year VI (9th June, 1798)
Ten o'clock in the evening

Order is given to depart at midnight to execute the landing in accordance with the instructions given on the 21st.

BONAPARTE

Ferdinand Von Hompesch (1744-1805)

To the Grand Master[I] of
the Order of Malta
On board *l'Orient*, 22 Prairial Year VI
(10th June, 1798)

Eminence, after having delivered, to the flagship, the response made by Your Eminence concerning the French request for water provisions, General Bonaparte takes exception to the fact that only four ships at a time will be allowed to enter the harbour. How much time will it take to replenish 600 vessels

---

[I] Ferdinand Von Hompesch

in this manner? The general finds your refusal all the more astonishing since he is aware of the preferential treatment given to the English by Your Eminence's predecessor.

General Bonaparte is determined to use force to obtain what he is rightfully entitled to, based on the principles of hospitality which are the essence of your Order's fundamental values.

I have seen the formidable force of General Bonaparte's army and I cannot see how the Order could possibly resist. In such grave circumstances it would have been more appropriate for Your Eminence to find a more amiable solution for the sake of the Order, its knights and the entire population of Malta.

The general did not want me to return from the flagship to a city which he now considers to be a traitor and enemy, whose only hope is to show loyalty to General Bonaparte He has given very specific orders to scrupulously respect the religion, and the property of the Maltese population.

June, 10, 1798 (old calendar)

Signed **Caruson**[1]

---

[1] French Consul of Malta

To Citizen Ganteaume,

Squadron Chief-of-Staff
On board *l'Orient*, 22 Prairial Year VI
(10th June, 1798) at midnight

Order to execute all the instructions related to the landing.

Citizen, I ask you to immediately order the frigate *la Diane* to disembark its men at the bay of Saint-Julien with the two 12-pounder mobile cannon and the artillery indicated in the instructions. You will also give the order to disembark from *l'Orient* a six-inch howitzer, and the artillery that goes with it.

You will order the *Timoleon* to immediately disembark a six-inch howitzer and the artillery indicated in the instructions. All the artillery must be landed at the bay of Saint-Julien as soon as possible.

By order of the general-in-chief

Elzéard August de Dommartin
(1768-1799)

To General Dommartin
On board *l'Orient*, 22 Prairial Year VI
(10th June, 1798) at midnight

Be aware Citizen General that I have given orders to have two 12-pounder cannon brought to the bay of Saint-Julien from *l'Orient*, as well as a six-inch howitzer from the *Timoleon*.

The general-in-chief wants you to take command of this artillery with a chief-of-battalion who will aim it against the fort on Point Dragut.

You will consult with General Caffarelli before deploying the artillery at different batteries making sure that they are not discovered until I give you further orders.

The general wants these batteries to be operational on the 25th He believes it is best to set up the batteries with barrels which you may find in the farmhouses. Your mission is to stop anyone from coming out of the fort and if possible, given the small number of artillery, you will try to silence the enemy fire.

The general wants you to act as soon as possible to force the enemy into early negotiations.

By order of the general-in-chief

General Vaubois
(1748-1838)

To General Vaubois

On board *l'Orient*, 23 Prairial Year VI
(11th June, 1798)

Citizen General, you have here a copy of an order which I have just given to Generals Caffarelli and Dommartin concerning the artillery that will be deployed against the fort at Point Dragut.

With regards to Citizen Marmont's brigade, the general wants to identify the best spots for the batteries such that we can tighten the blockade or attack the city fortifications.

Either way, you must immediately order a number of sappers from Marmont's brigade who will be paid to dig up earth to lead the enemy into believing that we are preparing batteries, defended with earth mounds or earth-filled barrels. This will give them cause for concern and will make them waste gunpowder if they are stupid enough to fire. That should help accelerate the negotiations.

It is of outmost importance that the city is completely blockaded such that nobody can leave or enter, and that you are able to communicate with General Desaix.

By order of the general-in-chief

To the Consul of the Batavian Republic[I] in Malta. On board *l'Orient*, 23 Prairial Year VI
(11th June, 1798)

Citizen Consul, the general-in-chief of the French Army on the shores of Malta has ordered me to inform you that the Order of Saint John of Jerusalem is now at war with the Republic of France. Given the alliance treaty between the French republic and the Batavian[II] republic, you will no longer exercise any authority with the said Order.

By order of the general-in-chief

[I] Count Agostino Formosa de Fremaux
[II] Dutch

To the Grand Master of the Order of Malta
On board *l'Orient*, 23 Prairial Year VI
(11ᵗʰ June, 1798)

Given that Your Excellence has requested the suspension of arms, the general-in-chief has ordered his *aide-de-camp*, chief-of-brigade, to pay you a visit. He is empowered to negotiate and sign the agreed suspension of arms.

I sincerely hope Your Excellence remains assured of the high esteem I have in his regard.

By order of the general-in-chief

To General Vaubois
On board l'Orient, 23 Prairial Year VI
(11ᵗʰ June, 1798)

General, the general-in-chief has been informed that the Grand Master of the Order of Jerusalem has signed a suspension of arms. The l'*Orient* is packed with envoys sent from every part of the city. If the suspension of arms is signed, it will apply only to the harbour cities unless other locations are clearly specified.

The general-in-chief hopes that you will be in control of the Old City and the rest of the island before the end of the day.

By order of the general-in-chief

Convention[I]
Concerning the handover of the city and the forts of Malta to the French
On board *l'Orient*, 24 Prairial Year VI
(12th June, 1798)

Signed between the republic, represented General-in-chief Bonaparte on one side, and the Order of the Knights of St. John of Jerusalem represented by MM. Bailli of Turin, Frisari, Commander Bosredon de Ransijat, Baron Mario Testaferrata, De Nicola Muscat, Advocate Benedetto Schembri and Councillor Bonanni, on the other. Under the mediation of his Catholic Majesty, the King of Spain, represented by Chevalier Felipe de Amat, his chargé d'affaires in Malta.

Article 1.
The Knights of the Order of St John of Jerusalem will surrender the city and the forts of Malta to the French army. All sovereign rights and properties of the islands of Malta and Comino are relinquished to the French Republic.

Article 2.
The French Republic will exercise its power of influence at the Congress of Rastadt to grant the Grand Master the lifetime possession of a principality equivalent to the loss he is incurring. In

---

[I] Doublet was present on l'*Orient* when Napoleon wrote this convention. He describes this event in great detail in his memoirs.

the meantime, it hereby engages to pay him an annual pension of 300,000 francs. He will also receive two years' worth of pension as compensation for his furniture. Until his departure from Malta, he will continue to retain all the military honours.

Article 3.
The French knights of the Order of St John of Jerusalem presently on Malta, whose status will be certified by the commander-in-chief, may return to their homeland. Their residency in Malta will be considered as a residency in France[1].

Article 4.
The French Republic grants the knights, presently in Malta, a lifetime pension of 700 francs. The pension is increased to 1,000 francs for the knights above the age of 60. The French Republic will do everything in its power to influence the Cisalpine, Roman, Ligurian, and Swiss Republics, to encourage them to make similar grants to their own knights.

Article 5.
The French Republic will exercise its influence on the other powers of Europe to allow their knights to continue exercising their legal rights on the Order's properties located in their States.

---

[1] Such that they would not be considered as émigrés

Article 6.

The knights will retain all their private properties on the islands of Malta and Gozo.

Article 7.

The inhabitants of Malta will be allowed to continue practising the Roman Catholic Apostolic Religion as in the past. They will keep their properties and the privileges they possess. They will not be subject to any special taxes.

Article 8.

All civil documents issued by the Government of the Order retain their validity and will be executed accordingly.

Made in duplicate on board the ship l'Orient moored at Malta, 24th Prairial, Year VI, of the French Republic (12th June, 1798).

- Le Commander Bosredon-Ransijat
- Il Barone Mario Testaferrata
- Il Dottor G. Nicolo Muscat
- Il Dottor Bened. Schembri
- Il Consign. V.F Bonnani, com
- Il Bali di Torini Frisari
- *(salvo diritto di alto dominio che appartiene*
- *al mio sovrano, come Re delle Due Sicilie)*
- El Caballero Felipe De Amat

Signed: **BONAPARTE**

Instructions
24 Prairial Year VI
(12th June, 1798)

Directives related to the convention concerning the handover of the city and the forts of Malta to the French

Following the articles agreed on the 24 Prairial (12th June) between the French republic and the Order of Malta the instructions are as follows:

Article 1.
Today, 24 Prairial (12th June) Fort Manoel, Fort Tigne, Fort St. Angelo, the edifices of Burmola, Cottonera and Vittoriosa will be handed over to the French troops.

Article 2.
Tomorrow, 25 Prairial (13th June) Fort Ricasoli, Fort St. Elmo, the edifices of the City of La Valette, Floriana and all the remaining edifices will be handed to French troops at midday.

Article 3.
French officers will visit the Grand Master today at 10 o'clock in the morning to give their orders to the governors of the forts and the edifices that are to be handed over to the French authorities. They will be accompanied by Maltese officers. There will be an officer for each of the forts to be handed over.

Article 4.

The same instructions as above will apply to the forts and edifices that are to be handed over to French authorities tomorrow, 25 Prairial.

Article 5.

The artillery, the stores and all charts are to be handed over at the same time as fortifications.

Article 6.

The troops of the Order of Malta are allowed to remain in their quarters until further notice.

Article 7.

The Admiral, commander of the French fleet will appoint an officer, today, to take possession of the boats, galleys and ships, as well as the arsenal and other belongings of the Order of Malta.

Signed:
- Il Bali di Torini Frisari
- Le Commander Bosredon-Ransijat
- Il Barone Mario Testaferrata
- Il Dottor G. Nicolo Muscat
- Il Dottor Bened. Schembri
- El Caballero Felipe De Amat

BONAPARTE

Order granting Bishop Labini
the use of the Church of St. John's
21 Prairial Year VI
(9th June, 1798)

To the Bishop of Malta[1]
24 Prairial Year VI
(12th June, 1798)

Monsieur l'Eveque[II], it gives me great pleasure to learn of your good conduct and the way you have welcomed the French troops. You can assure your dioceses that the Roman Catholic Apostolic religion will not only be respected but its clergy will receive special protection. I cannot think of any person more dignified or more worthy than a priest driven by the spirit of the Gospel who takes an oath of obedience to serve in the name of peace, serenity and union within a diocese. I would like *Monsieur l'Eveque* to go immediately to the city of Malta to use his influence to maintain peace and calm among the people. I will personally go there this evening. On my arrival, I would like you to introduce me to all your priests and the clergy heads of the city and of the surrounding villages.

Let me assure you, *Monsieur l'Eveque*, of my deepest desire to prove to you the high esteem and consideration I have in your regard.

BONAPARTE

---

[1] Bishop Vincenzo Labini
[II] Mr. Bishop

Bishop Vincenzo Labini

Letter from Renauld de Saint Jean d'Angely to Bishop Labini

City of La Valette 21 Messidor
Year VI (July 9, 1798)

From: Citizen Renauld de Saint Jean d'Angely.
Commisioner of the French Government for the
Island of Malta

71

To: *Monsieur l'Eveque*

Monsieur l'Eveque, as of today you may request the National Domain Commission, either directly or through of a person of trust, to be given the keys to Miari House[1]. The commission has received orders to make this house available for your use. Let me assure you, *Monsieur l'Eveque*, that you have my highest esteem.

Signed: The Government Commissioner

Renaud de Saint Jean d'Angely

---

[1] Valletta building to be used as the seminary

RÉPUBLIQUE FRANÇAISE.

à la Cité Valette Isle de Malte le 21 . *Mesndor* — an 6. de la République

Le Citoyen Regnaud de Saint Jean d'Angely Commissaire du
Gouvernement Français pour l'Isle de Malte.

A Monsieur L'Évêque de Malte .

Vous pouvez, Monsieur l'Évêque, demander, même
aujourd'hui, on faire demander par un homme de
confiance, la clef de la maison Miari, à la
Commission des Domaines Nationaux.
Cette Commission a reçu l'ordre de
tenir cette maison à votre disposition.
Recevez, Monsieur l'Évêque, l'assurance
de ma haute considération.

Le Commissaire du gouvernement

Regnaud de St Jean d'Angely.

Original copy of the letter to Bishop Labini

Order of the Day
24 Prairial Year VI
(12th June, 1798)

The army is informed that the enemy has surrendered. The flag of liberty has been raised on all the forts of Malta. The general-in-chief insists on rigorous discipline. The people and their property must be fully respected and you will be friendly towards the Maltese.

BONAPARTE

To Citizen Garat
Minister of the French Republic of Naples
Head Quarters of Malta, 25 Prairial Year VI
(13th June, 1798)

Citizen Minister, I am sending you a messenger on his way to Paris. Please provide him the necessary passports and send him safely on his mission.

I ask you to kindly inform the court of Naples in pure and simple terms about the occupation of Malta by French troops, about the sovereignty and the properties we have seized. You must also inform His Majesty King of the Two Sicilies that we intend to maintain the existing relations for the procurement of provisions as in the past. If we are not treated in the same way as you have treated Malta it will be considered an unfriendly gesture.

With regards to the sovereignty that the kingdom of Sicily exercises over Malta, we will not refute it as long as Naples recognises the sovereignty of the Roman Republic.

I am stopping here for two days to take water after which I will depart for the East. I do not know if you will remain in Naples for long. Please keep me informed about your intentions and send me news from Europe as often as possible.

You know the personal esteem and fondness I have for you.

BONAPARTE

P.S. To save time, I am sending my letter to directory using a *cachet volant*[1] so you may read it.

To the Executive Directory
Head Quarters of Malta, 24 Prairial Year VI
(12th June, 1798)

We arrived on the 21st at daybreak on the shores of Gozo. The convoy of *Civita-Vecchia* had arrived three days before. On the evening of the 21st I sent one of my *aide-de-camps* to the Grand Master to request water at different points around the island. The consul of the Maltese republic brought to me his response which was an outright refusal stating that he could allow only two boats at a time to come in. It is easy to calculate that it would take more than 300 hundred days to replenish the entire fleet. Given

---

[1] Light seal that does not prevent the letter from being opened

the army's urgent need, I had no choice but to use force to obtain water.

I ordered Admiral Brueys to prepare a landing. He sent Counter-Admiral Chayla with his squadron and the convoy of Civita-Vecchia to land his men at the bay of Marsa-Scirocco. The convoy of Genoa disembarked at Saint Paul's Bay and the Marseilles convoy landed on the island of Gozo.

General-of-brigade, Lannes, and Chief-of brigade, Marmont seized control of city's main gate. General Desaix and General Belliard landed with the 21st. He took control of all the batteries and all the forts along the coast of Marsa-Scirocco. By daybreak of the 22nd, our troops were in charge of all the points in spite of cannon attack which was very violent but extremely badly executed. On the evening of the 22nd, the city was surrounded and the rest of the island had surrendered. General Reynier had taken control of the island of Gozo, and General Baraguey-d'Hiller of the southern part of Malta after having captured several knights and two hundred men. General Desaix was within gunshot of the walls of Cottonera and Fort Ricasoli. He too captured several knights.

The poor inhabitants were completely terrified of what might happen. They sought refuge inside the city which became very crowded. Throughout the evening of the 22nd the city was vibrant with cannon fire. The besieged attempted a sortie but Chief-of-brigade Marmont, at the head of the 19th, captured the Order's flag.

On the 23rd I began to disembark the artillery. There are few places in Europe as well-fortified as Malta. I did not rely purely on military strength, I embarked on various negotiations and fortunately the outcome was positive.

The Grand Master sent an envoy on the 23rd in the morning to request a suspension of arms. I sent my *aide-de-camp*, Chief-of-brigade Junot, and authorized him to sign the capitulation with the Grand Master on the condition that he first surrendered the city. I sent citizen Poussielgue and Dolomieu to find out what the Grand Master and the Maltese had in mind.

On the 23rd at midnight the Grand Master's representatives came on board *l'Orient* and we finalized the convention which I am attaching. The Grand Master's representatives were headed by Commander Bosredon-Ransijat, a knight of the former Langue d'Auvergne. When he saw that they were taking up arms against us he immediately wrote to the Grand Master telling him that his duty as a knight was to fight the Turks and not his motherland and consequently refused to take part in the Order's unacceptable conduct. He was immediately imprisoned and was finally released so that he could take charge of the negotiations.

Yesterday, the 24th, we entered the city and took possession of all its forts. Today at midday we brought the fleet into the harbour.

I am particularly satisfied with Admiral Brueys and the unity and harmony which reign in his squadron. I also praise the zeal of Citizen Ganteaume's acts as chief-of-division of the main squadron. Frigate captain, Citizen Motard, commanded the landing boats. He is a young officer with a promising future.

On Malta we found two battleships, one frigate, 4 galleys, 1200 cannon, 1500 *livres* of powder, 40,00 muskets, etc. We will send you full details very shortly.

Enclosed are the orders I have given to establish the governing of this island.

Enclosed is the list of French residents in Malta, mostly knights who, one month before our arrival, had made donations to support the expedition to England.

I ask of you to promote Citizen Marmont to the grade of general-of-brigade.

BONAPARTE

Exposé on Malta's Conduct Regarding France during the Revolution

Head Quarters of Malta, 25 Prairial Year VI
(13th June, 1798)

From 1791 to 1795, this Order openly encouraged and authorised the knights who wanted to enlist in the army of *émigrés*. The *émigrés*, who sought refuge in Malta, even though they were not knights, were still allowed to join the Order in the name of honour. These *émigrés* include names like Narbonne-Fritzlar who was even received with great pomp.

In spite of the decree which classified the Order's French possession as state property, the Grand Master[1] continued to re-assign his fictitious commanderies when they became vacant. When Spain declared war on France, all Spanish warships were given open permission to recruit sailors from Malta. As many as 4000 muskets were given to the Spanish army following a request made by the court of Spain. Permission was also granted for the English to recruit from Malta. The Maltese government showed its utmost loyalty by declaring a punishment of three years in the galleys to anyone who violated their engagement.

In 1794, England's Viceroy of Corsica did not have enough powder to maintain control. He obtained 200 quintals from the government of Malta. Up to 1796, all French merchant ships were

---

[1] Emmanuel de Rohan-Polduc

79

forced to lower the national flag on entering the harbour. Last December, two French frigates, *la Justice* and *l'Artemise*, arrived at the port. Our consular agent tried in vain to obtain permission to recruit sailors. Meanwhile, two English Corsairs had no problem in doing so.

The partisans of the revolution were all persecuted, many of them exiled without formalities. In the month of May 1797, many were arrested and imprisoned like criminals.

Vassallo, one of the island's most learned and laudable persons was imprisoned for life.

As a result of all these facts, Malta became the enemy of France ever since the Revolution. It is through its own will that the island has been at war with France since 1793.

Collection of official letters published in year VIII by order of the premier consul.

Order

Bonaparte, general-in-chief, member of the National Institute, issues the following orders:

Article 1.
The island of Malta and Gozo will be administered by a government commission -consisting of nine persons who will be nominated by the general-in-chief.

Article 2.
Each member of the commission will take his turn at the presidency for a period of six months. The commission will appoint a secretary and a treasurer outside the commission.

Article 3.
The government commission will have a French commissioner.

Article 4.
The commission will be particularly responsible for the administration of the islands of Malta and Gozo and for receiving and managing all direct and indirect taxes. It will take the necessary measures related to the administration of this island. The health administration will come under its responsibility.

Article 5.
The chief commissioner will determine what it owes to the army as a monthly payment.

Article 6.
The government commission will immediately organize the tribunal for civil and criminal offences aligned as much as possible to that of France. The nomination of the members of the tribunal will require the approval of the division general of Malta. Until such a tribunal is formed, justice will continue to be administered as before.

Article 7.
The islands of Malta and Gozo will be divided into cantons the smallest of which will have a population of 3000 souls. The city of Malta will have two municipalities.

Article 8.
Each canton will be administered by a municipal body of five members.

Article 9.
Each canton will have its own magistrate.

Article 10.
The magistrate will be nominated by the government commission with the approval of Malta's commanding division-general.

Article 11.

The property of the Order of Malta, including that of the Grand Master and the knight's auberges belong to the French republic.

Article 12.

There will be a commission of three members who will carry out an inventory to administer the abovementioned assets. They will report to the chief commissioner.

Article 13.

The entire police force will take orders from the commanding division-general and his officers.

BONAPARTE

Order
Head Quarters of Malta, 25 Prairial Year VI
(13th June, 1798)

The general-in-chief issues the following orders:

Article 1.
With today's order I am appointing the members of the government organisation. The government commission is composed of the following citizens:

- Bosredon-Ransijat:
- Vincent Caruana: *Secretary to the bishop*
- Charles Asto: *Maltese merchant*
- Paolo Ciantar: *Maltese merchant*
- Jean-Francois Dorell: *Current deputy*
- Grongo: *Magistrate from Gozo*
- Benedetto Schembri: Magistrate
- Cannon Don Saverio Caruana[i]: *Artisan from Mdina*
- Christophe Frendo: *Notary*

Article 2.
Citizen Regnaud de Saint-Jean d'Angely is the government commissioner.

Artiicle 3.
Citizens Matthieu Poussielgue, Caruson and Roussel are the members of the commission

---

[i] Founder of a cotton textile factory in Malta [sic] Correspondence de Napoleon.

mentioned in Article 12 of the order of the day.

Article 4.
General Berthier will unite the members of the two commissions to officiate their oath of obedience to the republic before they officially take up their duties.

Article 5.
The government commission will name the two municipalities of Malta within 48 hours. The municipalities of Gozo will be named within five days.

BONAPARTE

Order
Head Quarters of Malta, 25 Prairial Year VI
(13th June, 1798)

The general-in chief issues the following orders:

Article 1.
The officers and soldiers of the military corps of the Order of Malta, such as the Malta Regiment, the Navy Corps, Infantry Corps, the Galley Corps, the guards deployed at the various forts as well the Grand Master's Guard, will assemble today at two o'clock in the afternoon. They will go to Bircarcara tomorrow at five o'clock in the morning and will be inspected by Brigade-General Lannes.

Article 2.

All representations of coat-of-arms will be destroyed within 24 hours. It is forbidden to wear family crests or any other distinctive symbol of nobility.

Article 3.

All knights and inhabitants that are subjects of a nation that is at war with France, such as Russia and Portugal, must leave Malta within 48 hours.

Article 4.

All knights under the age of sixty must leave the island within three days.

BONAPARTE

Annexe to the previous Order

Members of the Order who are exempted from expulsion by the general-in-chief

Ransijat:	Treasury Secretary
Fay:	Commissioner of fortifications and artillery officer
Breuvart:	Priest
Rouyer:	Former Grand Squire
Sandilleau:	Priest
Greicher:	Former chamberlain
Fim:	Priest
Dacia:	Servant d'armes
Beaufort:	Priest
Tousard:	Engineer
Lascaris:	The two brothers. One is insane, the other refused to take up arms against the army and asked to be locked up.
Gras:	Priest
Boeuf:	Priest
Doublet:	Secretary to the Grand Master

French

Most of whom provided me with useful information six months ago or made patriotic donations to support our expedition to England.

Medicis:	
Stendardi:	

Knights from Tuscany who made patriotic donation in support of our expedition to England.

Order
Head Quarters of Malta, 25 Prairial Year VI
(13th June, 1798)

The general-in-chief issues the following orders:
(exemptions from expulsion)

Article 1.
The knights who were not ordained and married in
Malta.

Article 2.
The knights who exercised a particular profession
on the islands of Malta.

Article 3.
Those who responsible for a manufacturing or
commercial establishment.

Article 4.
Finally, those listed in the above annexe, all of
whom are known for their good sentiments towards
the republic. They will be considered as Maltese
citizens and are entitled to remain in Malta as long
as they wish.

BONAPARTE

Order
Head Quarters of Malta, 25 Prairial Year VI
(13th June, 1798)

The general-in-chief issues the following order:

Article 1.
All items and merchandise belonging to English,
Russian, and Portuguese merchants will be sealed in
chests.

Article 2.
The consul of the republic is specifically responsible
for placing the seals.

BONAPARTE

To General Berthier
Head Quarters of Malta, 25 Prairial Year VI
(13th June, 1798)

You will order Monge and Berthollet to pay a visit
to the Mint, to the church of St. John and to any other
location that may contain precious objects.

BONAPARTE

Order
Head Quarters of Malta, 25 Prairial Year VI
(13th June, 1798)

The general-in-chief issues the following order:

Article 1.
Citizen Berthollet, the army's treasury controller and his accounts clerk will seize the gold, silver, and precious stones from the church of St. John and other locations that belonged to the Order of Malta, including the silver of the Grand master and that found in the auberges.
Article 2.
Throughout tomorrow, they will melt all the gold ingots and have it transported to the treasury of the army's paymaster.

Article 3.
The will carry out an inventory of all precious stones which will be placed under seal in the army's coffers.

Article 4.
They will sell 250,000 to 300,000 francs worth of silver to local merchants to obtain gold and silver coins which will go into the army's treasury.

Article 5.
The remaining silver will handed to the bursar who will leave it to the Mint of Malta to manufacture

coins that will be used to fund the troops. The use of this fund will be regulated such that the paymaster can he held accountable.

Article 6.
Any necessary items required to practice the religion will be left at the church of St. John and other churches.

BONAPARTE

To General Berthier

Head Quarters of Malta, 25 Prairial Year VI
(13th June, 1798)

Tomorrow at midday, General Berthier will assemble, at the municipality, all the municipal officers, the health magistrates, the police magistrates, all judges, the leading artisans, the heads of the Order, the priests, and finally all sorts of employees. They will take an oath of obedience to the French republic. He will draft a written declaration which must be signed by all.

BONAPARTE

To General Berthier

Head Quarters of Malta, 25 Prairial Year VI
(13th June, 1798)

Would you be kind enough, Citizen General, to send an officer to the various state prisons to liberate all those who were imprisoned because of their opinions.

BONAPARTE

To General Berthier

Head Quarters of Malta, 25 Prairial Year VI
(13th June, 1798)

Citizen General, Would you kindly give the order for the immediate liberation of a Neapolitan by the name of Laporte who was sentenced to the galleys because of his opinions.

BONAPARTE

To General Berthier
Head Quarters of Malta, 25 Prairial Year VI
(13th June, 1798)

You will order Division General Desaix to leave the forts and all the city locations under his command by tomorrow afternoon. His men will be replaced in the morning by the troops of General Vaubois. General Desaix will return to Marsa-Scirocco and continue to occupy the villages previously assigned to him. He must be ready to raise anchor on the 28th. General Vaubois will send the 19th to replace all the posts previously occupied by General Desaix.

You will inform him of my intentions to have the 19th and the 80th battalions and the 7th light-infantry remain on the island.

BONAPARTE

To the Directory of the Republic of Liguria
Head Quarters of Malta, 25 Prairial Year VI
(13 June, 1798)

Monsieur Chevalier Christophe Sauli is travelling to Genoa. He is one of the few knights whose political opinions are in line with those who currently govern the Republic of Ligura. I recommend him to you. I send you my regards

BONAPARTE

Comm. by the government of Sardinia.

To General Brune
Head Quarters of Malta, 26 Prairial Year VI
(14th June, 1798)

We have taken Malta my dear general. We have found 1200 cannon, two million *livres* of powder, two battleships, one frigate, four galleys, and 40,000 muskets. The minister of Naples, Garat, will give you the full details. I assume that you have taken the rest of the 79th and the 6th demi-brigade to Corfu.

With my regards.
BONAPARTE

To General Bonaparte
Malta, 25 Prairial Year VI
(13th June, 1798)

Following your orders I have visited various prisons to find out why subjects of Naples are being held in the Maltese prisons. It was not difficult to find out since they told me themselves that most of them are guilty of murder, theft and other crimes. Most of them would have already done their time had they remained in Naples but the conspiracy of Chevalier Medichy in 1795 caused great panic which is why the king of Naples decided to get rid of them by sending 500 of them to the prisons of Messina and 500 to Malta.

There are 700 Sicilian felons and 600 Turkish or Barbary slaves in the Maltese prisons. These men are worth a look since many of them could be useful to us. They are very willing to join the army as sailors. This is not surprising since the place in which they are locked up is atrocious. I have given orders to provide them with basic necessities and to make the place more hygienic.

DUPUY

To General Bonaparte
Malta, 25 Prairial Year VI
(13th June, 1798)

Rabato on the island of Gozo

Following your orders, I have taken possession of the island of Gozo on the 22nd of this month. The island was defended by a militia corps of local inhabitants. There were 800 musketeers, a coast-guard regiment of 1200 men and a company of 300 men, 30 of whom were on horseback. In total they had 2300 men deployed at the forts and batteries along the island's northern coast.

I decided not to land near their forts or batteries to avoid having to start hostilities and to protect our ships from the coastal batteries. I looked for an unguarded landing spot and went for *Redum Kebir*[1] between the new tower and the first battery at Ramla Bay. The inhabitants assumed that it was not possible to land there as the coast is extremely rugged. We scaled the heights along a passage formed by the streams.

The entire morning of the 22nd was spent uniting the convoy, sending signals and approaching the coast. The changing winds and the calm weather slowed us down considerably. At one o'clock in the afternoon I was with the convoy on *l'Alceste* at a distance of 800 to 900 *toises* from the coast. The calm weather stopped us from advancing further. To save time and to land before the enemy

---

[1] Rdum il-Kbir. Ramla il-Hamra, Gozo

could take up positions, I embarked my men on all the landing boats. I disembarked from the frigate *l'Alceste* with the 3rd grenadier company and the 85th demi-brigade. On seeing our advance, the enemy scrambled to occupy the heights. We rowed as hard as we could. The rock face was packed with country folk and a volley of shots rained on our landing boats as soon as we were within musket reach.

Citizen Bertrand, the grenadier sergeant-major, was hit and killed in my landing boat. The batteries of Ramla and *Terre-Neuve*[I] opened fire. I was on the landing boat of *l'Alceste* with General Fugière, your *aide-de-camp*, and the captains of the engineers, Geoffroy and Sabatier.

Two hundred men climbed up to the rock summit which dominates the coast where our boats were landing.

We climbed up the steep rubble-rock face as fast as possible almost without firing any shots, avoiding enemy fire and the rocks they hurled at us from above. Astonished by the perseverance of our grenadiers the enemy finally fled on seeing our first men reaching the summit.

The enemy and their batteries received a steady bombardment from *l'Etoile* and *le Pluvier*.

I united the troops at the top of Redum-Kebir. I marched with 85th demi-brigade towards the town of Chambray via Casal Nadur with the intention of taking the fort of Port Migiaro[II] to cut the link

---

[I] Dahlet Qorrot
[II] Mgarr Harbour

between Malta and Gozo.

At the same time I ordered the men from the 9th to march to the Gozo Castle via *Casal Sciara*[I]. Another detachment marched to the fort at *Mazzal-Formio*[II]. Fort Chambray was packed with local inhabitants who had taken refuge with their livestock. I made a proclamation to let them know of our intentions to avoid a futile retaliation attempt which could lead to terrible consequences. I left three companies on guard outside the fort and headed for the castle.

When the inhabitants of Rabato saw the French Troops they immediately surrendered and handed over the keys to the castle. The governor and the knights of Malta had fled and by the evening French troops were inside the castle of Gozo.

The proclamation I had made at Fort Chambray had a positive outcome and the drawbridge was raised. The inhabitants helped our troops enter the fort after which they returned to their homes with their livestock.

On the island we found 140 cannon, 40 of which were in Gozo Castle, 22 in Fort Chambray and the rest in other forts or coastal batteries. We also found a large number of muskets and three grain stores.

The armed inhabitants who had fled were not wearing uniforms and hence I took no prisoners. I felt it was better to treat them kindly to make sure they returned to their homes and to their daily tasks.

[I] Xaghara
[II] Marsalforn

Three of their wounded are in hospital.

The governor and the other knights of Malta were hiding. Some of them gave themselves up while others were captured. I have given them the freedom of Rabato until we know what fate awaits the knights of Malta.

I have maintained the island's civil and justice administration to be able to obtain what is needed for the troops. Each village has a syndicate that depends on a central administration based in Rabato. The island's governor was its fifth member and president. I have replaced him by another member who I chose from a list that was given to me by the other magistrates.

The population of Gozo has thirteen to fourteen thousand souls. Its cultivation is well-maintained but it produces mainly cotton which offers very little in terms of provisions for the troops. I hope there is enough livestock to provide the division with fresh meat during their stay. It is unlikely that there are enough sheep; the island has already run out of wine. There may be enough grain to make bread and biscuits for the garrison and the inhabitants but we are totally lacking in firewood for the furnaces. We need you to send us wood over from Malta. If we are going to stay for a while we need to obtain wood from Sicily or Lampedusa. We barely have enough straw or barley for the ships with horses.

The inhabitants are beginning to realize just how much they stand to benefit from our invasion.

Some of them were convinced that that we were going to give them the land that belonged to the Order of Malta. They even starting making claims on the best parcels of land. I had to put a stop to it. I made it clear that the farms and the land of the Order are now national property.

I await to receive new orders on how the island is to be administered before my departure once the convoy supplies are replenished.

REYNIER

The Landing by Citizen Marmont[1]

Being charged with the landing party of five battalions, three of the 4th light infantry, and two of the 19th of-the-line, we were the first to land on the island. A number of companies from the Maltese Regiment that were posted along the coast retreated immediately without a combat. We chased them as they sought refuge inside the city. I had the city covered from the sea up to the aqueduct, where we joined Desaix's corps that had already landed to the east side of the city. I advanced towards the city until I reached the ravelin of Floriana on the southern side of the city.

I posted my men as close as possible to tighten our attack. The drawbridge of the city was lowered, and a large number of troops came marching towards me in disarray. My men retreated slowly and in orderly fashion, firing occasionally to slow their advance. I ordered two battalions of the 19th, encamped at about gun-shot distance from the city, to prepare an ambush from both sides of the route, and to await further orders. My orders were carried

---

[1] Extract from Mémoires du maréchal Marmont, duc de Raguse de 1792 à 1841, Vol I page 358 by Auguste Frédéric Louis Viesse de Marmont (duc de Raguse)

out to the letter. On seeing my troops retreating, the Maltese advanced with confidence. Once they dominated our hiding spot, the 19th came out and met them with a deadly fire, which threw them in a state of great disarray. I advanced upon them with my troops, chased them with bayonets and killed many of them. I personally captured the flag of the Order which they carried at the head of the column. The poor Maltese soldiers, simple country folk that they are, spoke only Arabic and reasoned in this way: *"We are fighting the French and our commanders are also French. We have been defeated, therefore our commanders are traitors."*

In raging anger they massacred seven of their French knights. And yet, the French knights were the only ones willing to put up a fight. This incident did not bode well for French knights. They became so concerned for their safety; they sent a messenger the following day stating that if the negotiations underway did not lead to the surrender of the city they were prepared to hand me the keys to St. Joseph's Gate[1].

The Maltese were furious. At one point we were concerned about the signing of the capitulation as a number of Maltese country militia continued to occupy two of the forts inside the city. The forts in question are very high, tightly enclosed, and heavily armed cavaliers that dominate the entire city. They are known by the names of Saint John and Saint

---

[1] Portes des Bombes, Il-Bombi

James. The Maltese soldiers refused to give themselves up even after we had already entered the city. Had they persisted in resisting us only God knows what consequence we would have had to face given the position we were in.

MARMONT

To General Dugua
Head Quarters of Malta, 26 Prairial Year VI
(14th June, 1798)

Citizen General, would you kindly order the Grand Master's grenadiers to be ready to embark[1] tomorrow. They are to be treated and paid like French grenadiers.

You will order the soldiers of the infantry regiment to return home. The soldiers of the galley battalions will go to the arsenal where they will take orders from the navy commander. You will give the same order to the navy battalion. You will order the Malta Regiment to be ready to embark tomorrow.

BONAPARTE

---

[1] To Egypt

To General Berthier

Head Quarters of Malta, 26 Prairial Year VI
(14th June, 1798)

Citizen General, would you kindly order General Vaubois to have the 4th light-infantry replaced from the posts they currently occupy and to have them ready embark at Saint Paul's bay tomorrow. You will order General Vaubois to send a detachment of 200 men to the island of Gozo before the departure of General Reynier's division. You will order General Reynier to embark on the 28th and to bring his convoy on the 29th to patrol outside the harbour without entering. You will order the various detachments of the 41st in the squadron to disembark to form part of the Malta garrison. Tomorrow you will embark the three grenadier companies of the 18th and the 32nd as well as the four companies of the 25th. These troops will board the same vessels they had disembarked from. The three grenadier companies of the 19th and 1st battalions will also go to St. Paul's bay tomorrow to embark on the Corsican convoy. The 2nd and 3rd battalions will remain on Malta until further orders.

The garrison of Malta will therefore consist of:

7th demi-brigade	900 men
6th of the line	518
41st of the line	285
80th of the line	650
19th of the line (2nd battalion)	700
Total	3053

And five artillery companies

104

You will give orders to have all the sick men in the squadrons, and in the various convoys, to be taken to the hospital of Malta. On the 28th you will embark the foot-guides, 200 on *l'Orient* and the rest on the *William Tell*.

The ships previously used for the guides will now be at the disposition of General Baraguey d'Hilliers. The remaining ships staying at Malta that carried the two battalions of the 19th will be used to embark the 4th light-infantry.

BONAPARTE

To General Berthier
Head Quarters of Malta, 26 Prairial Year VI
(14th June, 1798)

Citizen General, would you kindly send orders, via the frigate *la Sensible* which departs this evening, to the three fusilier companies of the 23rd infantry demi-brigade and to the various Corsican companies that are embarking at Porto-Vecchio, to sail to Malta escorted by the frigate *la Badine* where they will receive further orders.

You will also give orders to Citizen Belleville, consul of Genoa, to the commander of Civita-Vecchia and to other commanders from Toulon, to send to Malta their men of their various army corps.

BONAPARTE

To General Berthier

Head Quarters of Malta, 26 Prairial Year VI
(14th June, 1798)

Chief-of-brigade Bessieres, commander of the mounted guides is ordered to take the company of foot guides under his command. Consequently, Adjutant-General Boyer will transfer his company and will make sure they obey the orders they are given.

After taking command of these two corps, Citizen Bessieres, will appoint Chief-of-Battalion Dupas under his command to take charge of the foot guides. He will make sure to have them wear the same colours as the mounted guides as soon as possible. He will announce to the corps that the more trust he has from the general-in-chief the more severe he will be in maintaining discipline.

He will insist upon them that the foot guides and the mounted guides must set an example with regards to discipline and demonstrate the utmost audacious bravery. It is their duty to report any of their fellow soldiers who lack such qualities and therefore not worthy of being among them.

By order of the general-in-chief

Comm. by M. Duke of Istria

Order of the Day
Head Quarters of Malta, 26 Prairial Year VI
(14th June, 1798)

All troops, with the exception of those who received orders to remain on Malta, must be ready to depart immediately on receiving the order. The squadron must be rigged and ready to depart imminently. The generals will ensure that nobody disembarks without permission.

By order of the general-in-chief

To the Government Commissioners of Corcyra[I], Ithaca[II] and the Department of the Aegean Sea
Head Quarters of Malta, 27 Prairial Year VI
(15th June, 1798)

I am informing you Citizen, that the flag of the republic is flying on all the forts of Malta and that the Order of Malta has been destroyed. I will very shortly be informing you about the direction that the army will take. Tell the inhabitants of your department what is happening; they will reap all the benefits. Do not miss any opportunity to also inform the Greeks of Morea[III] and other parts.

BONAPARTE

[I] Corfu
[II] Short-lived French department in present-day Greece
[III] Peloponnese peninsula in Southern Greece

To the General Commander of Corfu[I]
Head Quarters of Malta, 27 Prairial Year VI
(15th June, 1798)

We entered Malta three days ago, Citizen General. In doing so, the republic has acquired a base that is extremely well-fortified and in an ideal location for our commerce. The inhabitants of your three departments are particularly well-placed to take full advantage. Announce the good news to them. I will leave General Vaubois to take command of Malta. You may correspond with him for any items you may require.

Your division forms part of the army under my command. I ask you to please send a brig with the exact details on the situation of your troops, your navy, the ammunition and your food supply. Let me know also if you are able to recruit sailors to board the ship and the frigate that are currently in Corfu and the have them sent to me at a designated location.

Please transmit the news of the occupation of Malta by the French army to our Ambassador in Constantinople. Inform him about the destruction of the Order of Saint-John-of-Jerusalem. Inform also Ali-Pasha, the Pasha of Scutari[II] and the Pasha of Morea. I want you to send only a commerce boat to Constantinople.

[I] Division-general Chabot
[II] A district of present-day Istanbul

108

The *chebek[1]*, *Le Fortunatus* has been ordered to join the squadron, have her accompanied by one of your best brigs so that I can sent her back to you with new orders. Be prepared for a Turkish attack. There is no point in letting them know where the army is heading.

BONAPARTE

P.S Send me news about the countries neighbouring your territory

Comm. by M. Garnier

---

[1] Small Mediterranean boat

Order

Bonaparte, member of the National Institute, General-in-chief orders:

- The Citizens of the Order of Jerusalem
- Marc-Antoine Saint-Exupéry
- Joseph La Panouse
- Jean-François-Alexandre Borassol
- Paul-Victor Hebrail, *on board le Causse*
- Henri-César Vibrac
- Isidore-David Beauregard
- Hippolyte-David Beauregard
- Jean-Durand Sartous
- Célestin Saint-Félix
- Jean de La Faye
- Joseph-Balthasard de Pierre
- Guillaume Sainte-Colombe
- Scipion du Roure-Brizon
- Jean-Chrysostome-Antoine Rebourg
- Philippe-Charl-Gabriel La Bègue
- Charles-Louis Budes de Guêbriant
- Eorges-Marie-René Cheffontaine
- Charles-François-August de Bonvouloir
- Anne-Guy Desescotais
- Hippolyte Saint-Victor
- Jean-Baptiste Duchesne de Saint Léger
- Gédéon Janvre
- Louis-Auguste Daurai Saint-Poix
- Jean-Baptiste Jemieu de Lescours, *sent by the general-in-chief to be included on the list.*

- Charles-François Dandigé, *sent by the general-in-chief to be included on the list.*
- Louis-François-Simon Pina, *sent by Sulkowski*
- François-Charles La Panouze, *on board le Causse*
- André-Louis Saint Simon, *on board le Tonnant*
- Gabrielle Melville, *on board le Causse*
- René-Joseph Dupeyroux, *board le Causse*
- Louis-Auguste Bourbel, *on board le Causse*
- Hippolyte Bernis, *on board le Causse*
- Charles Saint-Chamant, *on board le Causse*

to be taken on board to join the army as volunteers

BONAPARTE

To the French Consuls in Tunis, Tripoli
Head Quarters of Malta, 27 Prairial Year VI
(15th June, 1798)

I am informing you Citizen that the Republican Army is in possession of the city and the two islands of Malta and Gozo since two days. The French flag flies on all the forts. Would you be kind enough to inform the Bey about the destruction of the Order of Malta and about the republic's new possession. Could you inform him that from now on he must treat the Maltese with respect since they are now French subjects. I would like you also to ask him to liberate all Maltese slaves that he may have. I have given orders to liberate more than 2000 Barbary and Turkish slaves kept on galleys by the Order of Saint-

111

John-of-Jerusalem.

Make it known to the Bey that Malta has become significantly more powerful in the last three or four days and is in a position to punish him should he deviate for one moment from the respect that he owes to the republic.

BONAPARTE

To the Executive Directory
Head Quarters of Malta, 28 Prairial Year VI
(16th June, 1798)

The fleet is beginning to sail out of the harbour and on the 30th we expect all ships to be on the way to our destination. I have left the island under the command of General Vaubois; he was in charge of the landing and he appeased the local inhabitants with his kindness and wisdom.

The Grand Master leaves tomorrow for Trieste. Of the 600,000 francs we granted him, he will leave behind 300,000 to settle his debts. This sum will be over and above the land of the Order that we now own. I gave him 100,000 francs in cash and the paymaster gave him four bills of exchange of 500,000 francs each, totalling 2,000,000 francs. I ask you to give orders to have them settled. All the silver on the island including that of Saint-John will total to less than a million. I will keep this money to meet the expenses of the garrison and for the completion of the ship *le Saint-Jean*.

Enclosed you have the names[1] I have given to the two ships, the frigate and the galleys we have found here. You will also find a copy of the various orders I have given. I have not left out anything that is important for us to keep this island. I ask you to send over the rest of the 7th infantry demi-brigade as well as the 80th and the 23rd which is currently in Corsica. We need a good solid corps over here. Nothing is more important than this base. It is in excellent condition and well looked after but the fortifications are very extensive.

I ask you to send over all the men of our demi-brigades that remained behind. There should be several thousand. Malta could use four companies of foot artillery. I have embarked all the Turkish slaves of Malta as sailors. They will be very useful.

The number of knights in Malta totals 300. Those over sixty will be allowed to stay. I am taking with me all those who are under thirty. The rest will go to Antibes and those who did not take up arms against France can return home as specified in Article 3 of the capitulation.

BONAPARTE

---

[1] This list was never found (Correspondence de Napoleon)

THE REFORMS

Order
Head Quarters of Malta, 28 Prairial Year VI
(16th June, 1798)

The general-in-chief issues the following orders:

Article 1.
All the inhabitants of Malta are equal in right. They are distinguished only by their talent, their merit, their patriotism, and their loyalty to the French republic.

Article 2.
Slavery is abolished. All slaves known by the name of *bonavogli* will be freed and the contracts that bind them, shameful to the human species, will be destroyed.

Article 3.
In view of the previous article, all the Turkish slaves belonging to individuals will be handed over to the commander general and will be treated like prisoners of war. Given the friendly relations between Ottoman Porte and the French Republic, they will be sent home as soon as the general-in-chief gives the order, but only after he receives confirmation that the Bey accepts to send to Malta all their French and Maltese slaves.

Article 4.
All the inhabitants of Malta and Gozo must wear the tri-coloured cockade. No Maltese can wear the French National costume without special permission from the general-in-chief. The general-in-chief will grant the title of French citizen and the permission to wear the national costume to those Maltese that distinguish themselves through their loyalty to the republic, by a special deed, donations, or through an act of bravery.

Article 5.
Ten days after publication of the present order, it is forbidden to display coat-of-arms inside or outside houses, or to seal letters using crests, or to expect feudal privileges.

Article 6.
Given that the Order of Malta is dissolved, it is strictly forbidden to use the titles of bailiff, commander, or knight.

Article 7.
Ten days after publication of this order, it is strictly forbidden to wear the uniform of the corps of the former Order of Malta.

Article 8.
Every church will replace the Grand Master's crest with that of the French Republic.

Article 9.
As Malta now belongs to the French Republic, the missions of all its plenipotentiary ministers are terminated.

Article 10.
All foreign consuls will cease to exercise their functions until they receive new credentials form their government to continue their service in the city of Malta which has now become a French port.

Article 11.
All foreigners living in Malta are obliged to conform to the present order no matter what rank or grade they carry in their country of origin.

Article 12.
Any breach of the above articles will be punishable by a fine of a third of their income for a first offence, three months in prison for a second offence, and deportation from Malta and the confiscation of half of their goods for a fourth offence. There must always be an interval of 10 days between each offence.

BONAPARTE

Order

The general-in-chief issues the following orders:

Article 1.
There will be a general disarmament of all the inhabitants of the islands of Malta and Gozo. Arms will be permitted only by permission of the commanding general to men who are known for their patriotism.

Article 2.
The infantry volunteers of Malta and Gozo will be maintained. However, this corps will consist only of men on whom we can rely. We will make sure to only appoint officers who are patriotic.

Article 3.
Signals will be re-established from the tip of Gozo to Malta.

Article 4.
The laws of the health department of Malta will be not more nor less rigorous than those of Marseilles.

Article 5.
A company of 30 volunteers will be formed consisting of young men between 15 and 30 years of age. They will be selected from the richest families.

Article 6.

The division-general will make his selection for the above-mentioned company and inform the government commission within ten days. The government commission will enlist them and ten days after they must be in uniform with sword. They will wear the same uniform as the army guides but with aiguillettes[1] and a white button.

Article 7.

Anyone missing from the inspection of the division-general will be punished; the young men with one year in prison and their parents with a fine of 1000 ecus.

Article 8.

The government commission will designate sixty young men from the richest families. They will be sent to Paris to study in the colleges of the republic. Their parents must provide them with a living allowance of 800 Francs and 600 Francs for their voyage. They will make the voyage on battleships.

Article 9.

The government commission will send the names of these young men to the general-in-chief at the latest within 20 days. They will wear blue jacket and trousers but with red facings and cuffs and white borders. They will disembark at Marseilles where

---

[1] Braided cords

the interior minister will give orders to have them placed in national schools.

Article 10.
The commissioner in charge of the navy will appoint six young Maltese from the richest families to receive naval training and will have access to all grades.

Article 11.
Given that education is so important for prosperity and for public safety, those parents who refuse to enlist their designated children will have to pay a fine of 1000 ecus.

Article 12.
Classes for sailors will be established as in the French ports. When a squadron needs sailors and there are not enough volunteers, we will give preference to young men between 15 and 25 years old. If that does not suffice we will take men between the ages of 25 and 35 and finally those between 35 and 45.

BONAPARTE

Order

Head Quarters of Malta, 28 Prairial Year VI
(16th June, 1798)

The general-in-chief issues the following orders:

Article 1.
Each municipality in the city will have a National Guard battalion consisting of 900 men in uniform; green jacket, red facings cuffs and borders, with white piping. The National Guard will be selected from among the richest men, merchants and those who are most concerned by public safety.

Article 2.
They will provide all the necessary guards and patrols for the police on a daily basis; they will never be used for guarding forts.

Article 3.
The Infantry Corps will be maintained.

Article 4.
The division-general will establish the rules for organizing the National Guard and the infantry service. Both will receive the quantity of arms they require for the service.

Article 5.
Four veteran companies will be formed of elderly soldiers who served under the Order of Malta and

who are incapable of taking an active role. The first two of these companies will be sent to join the garrison at Corfu. This article will be carried out at all cost regardless of any difficulties encountered. I have no intention of keeping such a huge number of men accustomed to the ways of the Order of Malta.

Article 6.
Four companies of gunners will be formed similar to the one that already existed before. They will be deployed on the coastal batteries. Each of these companies will include French gunners, an officer and a French non-commissioned officer.

Article 7.
Any individual wishing to form a company of 100 infantry can do so. As soon as the company is established with its officers, it will be sent to join the army.

BONAPARTE

Order
Head Quarters of Malta, 28 Prairial Year VI
(16th June, 1798)

The general-in-chief issues the following orders:

Article 1.
All French troops on Malta will wear cotton uniforms. Each corps is responsible for making its own uniforms. Their equipment will be repaired.

Article 2.

If we cannot find blue cotton, they can wear white cotton with red and blue collar and facings such that they always wear the three colours.

Article 3.

The first corps to need equipment repairs is the 19th battalion and after that it is the battalion of the 7th light-infantry.

Article 4.

The division-general will consult with the government commission to take the necessary measures, even the most severe, to ensure that the barracks of the Malta garrison has all the provisions required by the law. Their services will be kept to a minimum and hence the city is to be guarded by the National Guard.

Article 5.

The division-general will provide the necessary troops to the navy commander to guard the arsenal.

Article 6.

At least once every six months the division-general will pay a visit to the island of Gozo to spend time with the inhabitants, to talk to them, to ensure that the commanding officers are not doing anything that might irk them and to reprimand any abuse. At least once a month, the division-general will do a tour visit around the island of Malta.

Article 7.
The best hospital, the one used by the knights, will be reserved exclusively for the French.

BONAPARTE

Order
Head Quarters of Malta, 28 Prairial Year VI
(16th June, 1798)

The general-in-chief issues the following orders:

Article 1.
All priests and nuns that are not from Malta or Gozo, regardless of which order they belong to, must leave the island at the latest ten days after publication of the present order. Only the bishop, given his pastoral role, is exempt from this order.

Article 2.
Any clerical vacancy created by the present order will be filled by Maltese given that it is unjust that foreigners should reap the benefits of this country.

Article 3.
It is not allowed to take religious vows before the

age of thirty. No new priest will be ordained until all existing priests are employed.

Article 4.

Malta and Gozo can have no more than one convent or monastery for each religious order. The government commission will consult with the bishop to agree upon which location is to be retained for each order. All belongings that are no longer required from the vacant edifices will be given to the poor. All private foundations, secular convents, penitent groups, and collegial organisations are banned. The cathedral will have 15 cannon deployed at the city of Valletta and five cannon at Mdina.

Article 5.

It is formally forbidden for a lay person who is not at least a deacon to wear a collar and robes.

Article 6.

The bishop is required, within ten days of the publication of this order, to report on the status of all priests with the certificates to prove they are nationals of Malta or Gozo. Those who do not meet the requirement stipulated in the order will be required to leave the island. Any individual who does not respect the present order will be sentenced to six months in prison.

Article 7.

The government commission, its commissioner and the division-general are in charge of making sure that this order is carried out.

BONAPARTE

Order

Head Quarters of Malta, 28 Prairial Year VI
(16th June, 1798)

The general-in-chief issues the following order:

Article 1.

The division-general, the navy commissioner and the government commissioner will unite to identify a location for a new quarantine hospital.

Article 2.

Merchant ships and foreigners will continue to use the existing quarantine hospital[1].

Article 3.

The new quarantine hospital will include an open space 400 *toises* long and 400 *toises* wide and will have a number a country manors or mansions. It must be big enough to house 500 to 600 soldiers with special quarters for a general and several senior officers. It must have a nice country house with a beautiful garden. It will be used for quarantine

---

[1] Based on Manoel Island

purposes but also for convalescing soldiers who have to be repatriated to France.

Article 4.
We will choose the location in exchange of national property.

BONAPARTE

To Citizen Najac

Head Quarters of Malta, 28 Prairial Year VI
(16th June, 1798)

It has been a while since you received news from us. You should have, however, received the two dispatch boats I sent you. Since my departure from Toulon I have received only a brig that had left 48 hours after us. After two days of musket and cannon fire we have taken Malta and all its forts. We have found two battleships, one frigate, four galleys, 1500 to 1800 cannon and 40,000 muskets. As far as the arsenal is concerned, it is not well stocked.

I am sending you *la Sensible* with the Ambassador of the republic of Constantinople on board. I hope that the three Venetian ships are in good shape thanks to you, and that all the troops that were left behind can depart shortly under their escort. Send to Malta everything that is destined for us. I want these ships to escort all the troops that the consul of Genoa can send us. I ask you to send over two dispatch boats from Toulon to Malta each month; the naval commissioner will forward our mail to us wherever we are.

BONAPARTE

To Citizen Le Roy
Head Quarters of Malta, 28 Prairial Year VI
(16th June, 1798)

The general-in-chief has given orders to Admiral Brueys to identify the Turkish slaves who could be deployed on board our ships. Could you give orders on behalf of Admiral Brueys or the navy Chief-of-staff Ganteaume to make available to them all the Turkish salves that are in the prisons. There should be about 500 of them. You will decide with Admiral Brueys on which ships they will board and the necessary security measures.

By order of the general-in-chief

To the Executive Directory
Head Quarters of Malta, 29 Prairial Year VI
(17th June, 1798)

You will find enclosed, the original treaty which the Order of Malta has just agreed upon with Russia. It was signed only five days ago. It is the same document I had intercepted in Ancona two years ago before it was sent. As such, His Majesty the Emperor of Russia should thank us since our occupation of Malta will save him 400,000 roubles. We know exactly what they were planning. Nevertheless, if he was intending to pave the way for the mooring of his fleet in the port of Malta, he should have done so more discretely and not be so open about it. Either way, we now have in our possession the strongest base in the Mediterranean and it is going to be very costly to try and dislodge us.

BONAPARTE

To General Dommartin, Artillery Chief
Head Quarters of Malta, 29 Prairial Year VI
(17th June, 1798)

General, I inform that the general-in-chief wants to send to Paris the 4-calibre cannon that is in the arsenal. It is worth keeping for its good workmanship. Could you bring it on board *la Sensible* today as it departs tonight. General Baraguey will take care of transporting it to Paris along with the Maltese flags.

By order of the general-in-chief

To the King of Spain

Head Quarters of Malta, 29 Prairial Year VI
(17th June, 1798)

The Republic of France has accepted the mediation of His Majesty for the capitulation of Malta. Chevalier de Amati, your representative in Malta has shown himself amiable to both the French republic and the Grand Master. However, since the port of Malta is now occupied by the republic, the post held by M. de Amati has been suppressed. I urge His Majesty to bear this in mind when he grants his special favours.

I ask His Majesty to trust in the respect and the high esteem I have for him.

BONAPARTE

Order
Head Quarters of Malta, 29 Prairial Year VI
(17th June, 1798)

The general-in-chief issues the following order:

Article 1.
The women and children of the Grand Master's grenadiers and of the soldiers of the Malta regiment

will receive an allowance each *decade*[I]; women will receive 20 *sous*[II], children 10 *sous*.

Article 2.
All male children under the age of 10 will be taken on board the vessels of the republic as cadets.

Article 3.
The paymaster will retain 1 *sou* and 1 *denier*[III] from the pay of the grenadiers and soldiers with children.

Article 4.
The wives of non-commissioned officers will receive 30 *sous* per decade and their children under the age of ten will receive 15 *sous*.

Article 5.
The sum will be retained from their husband's wages.

Article 6.
The government commission will ensure that this order is carried out.

BONAPARTE

[I] 10 days
[II] Former unit of French currency
[III] Worth less than 1 sou

Order
Head Quarters of Malta, 29 Prairial Year VI
(17th June, 1798)

The general-in-chief issues the following order:

Article 1.
Latin priests are no longer allowed to officiate in Greek churches.

Article 2.
The masses previously celebrated by Latin priests in Greek churches will now be celebrated in other churches.

Article 3.
Protection will be given to Jews who wish to establish a synagogue.

Article 4.
The commander general thanks the Greek inhabitants of Malta for their good conduct during the siege.

Article 5.
All the Greeks on the islands of Malta and Gozo, in Itahque, Corcyra, and in the departments in the Aegean Sea, who maintain relations with Russia, will be sentenced to death.

Article 6.

Any Greek ship flying the Russian flag will be attacked by French ships and will be sunk.

BONAPARTE

To General Berthier

Head Quarters of Malta, 29 Prairial Year VI
(17th June, 1798)

Citizen General, enclosed is the list of French Knights of Malta present on the island on our arrival. You will pass it on to the minister chief-of-police with instructions, following my orders, to issue each one with a passport to Antibes. They will receive no favourable or unfavourable treatment.

According to the capitulation convention, the knights who are currently on the island must be considered as having resided in France, and those knights who left France only to come to Malta and did not take up arms against the republic must be considered as French.

You will inform the minister that some of the 300 knights are over the age of sixty and they are allowed to remain on Malta. Those below the age of 26 I am taking with me. Finally, a small number of them who are guilty of having taken up arms against the republic will not be allowed to return. Consequently the number of 300 will be reduced by half.

You will inform the knights that the commander-in-chief has been given orders to give each one of them 150 *livres* for their voyage.

BONAPARTE

To General Berthier
Head Quarters of Malta, 29 Prairial Year VI
(17 June, 1798)

Citizen General, you will give orders in Toulon for all army wives who remained behind will embark on the convoy ship that will bring them to Malta where they will receive new orders for their next destination. You will carry out these instructions tomorrow as ordered by the army.

BONAPARTE

To the Executive Directory
Head Quarters of Malta, 30 Prairial Year VI
(18th June, 1798)

General Baraguey d'Hilliers brings you the great flag of the Order and that of many Maltese regiments. This officer was forced to return to Paris for health reasons. He always showed exemplary conduct with the army of Italy and carried out missions I assigned to him with great success.

I am sending you a copy of the latest order I have given for the administration of the island. Among them you will find the orders concerning public education. I am asking you to send three students from the polytechnic, one to teach arithmetic and geometry, the second to teach algebra and the third to teach mechanics and physics. They will be lodged and well-paid.

You will find enclosed some of the best panoramic views of Malta. I am also sending a silver galley. It is a model of the first galley of the Order from Rhodes. I found it interesting given its age. You also have a Chinese table-top tray which was used by the Grand Master for his ceremonies. It is remarkably well made.

BONAPARTE

Order
Head Quarters of Malta, 30 Prairial Year VI
(18th June, 1798)

Article 1.
The government commission will be divided into a bureau and a council.

Article 2.
The bureau will be composed of three members including a president.

Article 3.
Every six months the council will designate one of the two members of the bureau.

Article 4.
The bureau will provide a permanent service and each member will receive a salary of 4000 Francs.

Article 5.
The council will meet only once each *decade* to stay informed as to what the bureau is doing.

Article 6.
Council members will receive a salary of 1000 Francs per year.

Article 7.
The member of the bureau for this time will be N..... N.....[I] for a period of six months, and Citizen N..... for one year.

Article 8.
The government commissioner will receive a salary of 6000 Francs, apart from covering his bureau expenses; he will also receive a special grant for his transfer.

BONAPARTE

[I] Person to remain unnamed

Order

Article 1.
No ships can enter or leave the harbour without the order of the division-general commander of the island and its ports.

Article 2.
The government commission is responsible for setting up the civil, legal and administrative structures.

Article 3.
It cannot act without the commissioner's approval. The commissioner must be included in all the commission's deliberations and his opinions taken into account.

Article 4.
No regulation will be published or executed without the prior approval of the commissioner and the division-general.

Article 5.
The lands commission is responsible for creating an inventory of all the properties and assets belonging to the republic as well as for the administration of all national possessions.

Article 6.

It will submit the inventory lists, including new acquisitions, to the government commission every month.

Article 7.

No assets or properties may be sold without the permission of the general-in-chief. Should the need to generate emergency funds arise, the government commissioner, the division-general, the war commission and the commission members will congregate to prepare a declaration which will allow the sale of up to 150,000 Francs. The government commissioner will be in charge of setting the regulations and to respect every detail.

Article 8.

The lands commission will use the same paymaster as the military division who keep a special register and a separate fund for its assets.

Article 9.

Only the island's commanding general has the right to interfere with the administration of the country. The commanding generals that are under his command as well as the commanding officers of the city, and military agents, will in no manner interfere with administrative matters. The commanding general can never be represented by one of his subordinates.

BONAPARTE

Order
Head Quarters of Malta, 30 Prairial Year VI
(18th June, 1798)

Bonaparte, the general-in-chief issues the following order:

Article 1.
The commissioners of the land commission will receive a yearly salary of 4000 Francs.

Article 2.
Those who are not already resident in the country will receive a grant of 2000 Francs to support their moving expenses.

Article 3.
A sum of 6000 Francs will be granted by the lands department to the government commissioner for his move. The first 3000 will be paid immediately and the second 3000 will be paid in six months.

Article 4.
The annual lodging and bureau expenses of the commission must not exceed the sum of 12,000 to 15,000 Francs.

BONAPARTE

Order

Article 1.
The existing taxes will be temporarily maintained. They will be received by the government commissioner and the administrative commission.

Article 2.
A new taxation system will be established as soon as possible such that the revenues from customs, wine, stamps, tobacco, registers, salt, house rents and servants will amount to 720,000 Francs.

Article 3.
From these taxes, a monthly sum of 50,000 Francs will go to the army paymaster's treasury. This payment will begin only in three months' time, until then it will be handled by the treasury of lands department.

Article 4.
The remaining 120,000 Francs will be retained to cover the administrative costs, justice, etc…

Article 5.
The government commission and the commissioner of the republic will allocate the funds once the tribunal and the various administrative services are in place.

Article 6.
Street paving, lighting and cleaning will be paid by the inhabitants.

Article 7.
The maintenance of water fountains and the salaries of the men in charge of their upkeep will be paid from a levy charged to the ships that take water.

Article 8.
Road maintenance will be covered by a toll charge.

Article 9.
Public education will paid from existing assets. If that does not suffice, we will use the funds generated by the sale of suppressed convents as per previous order from the general-in-chief.

Article 10.
The salary and expenses of the health magistrates will be paid by a tax imposed on ships and on travellers.

Article 11.
The *Monte di Pietà*[I] will be maintained. The government commission will be responsible for its new structure.

[I] Pawn service administration of Malta

Article 12.

The establishment known as *l'università,* responsible for grain imports, will be maintained with a new administration starting from *Messidor 1.* The government commission will reorganize it such that the republic should never have to worry about the island's provisioning.

Article 13.

The hospitals will be restructured and funded from the sales of suppressed convents and monasteries. Existing hospitals will be maintained.

Article 14.

The postal system will be organized such that it can be funded by a letter-tax.

Article 15.

The funds available in those three months, during which the government pays nothing to the army, will be used to cover the costs of setting up the government and to cover army-related expenses.

Article 16.

The government commissioner is temporarily authorised to settle any unforeseen expenses. He will report such cases to the general-in-chief.

BONAPARTE

Order
Head Quarters of Malta, 30 Prairial Year VI
(18th June, 1798)

General-in-chief Bonaparte issues the following order:

Article 1.
Malta will have a central school which will replace the existing university and other academies.

Article 2.
It will be composed of:

- A teacher of arithmetic and *stereometry* with a salary of 1800 Francs
- A teacher of algebra and s*tereometry* with a salary of 2000 Francs.
- A teacher of geometry and astronomy with a salary of 2,400 Francs.
- A teacher of mechanics and physics with a salary of 3000 Francs
- A teacher of navigation with a salary of 2400 Francs.
- A teacher of chemistry with a salary of 1200 Francs.
- A teacher of oriental languages with a salary of 1200 Francs

---

I Study of volume and capacity

Article 3.
The following establishments will come under the central school:

- The library and the antiques department.
- The natural history museum.
- The botanic garden.
- The observatory.

Article 4.
A fund of 3000 Francs will be set aside for the school's equipment and maintenance.

Article 5.
The teachers will form a council responsible for the improvement of teaching methods. The council will make its proposals to the government commission.

Article 6.
The teacher's salaries, the wages of those employed by the government commission, and the administration costs of the various establishments, will be paid form the funds allocated to the *università* and the academy of oriental languages.

Article 7.
The botanic garden will be granted a piece of land of 30 acres. The land will be chosen without delay by the government commission and will be as fertile and as close to the city as possible.

Article 8.

The officers of the city hospital will organize a course in anatomy and child birth.

BONAPARTE

Order

Head Quarters of Malta, 30 Prairial Year VI
(18th June, 1798)

General-in-chief Bonaparte issues the following order:

Article 1.

Fifteen primary schools will be created in Malta and Gozo.

Article 2.

The pupils will be taught reading and writing in French, basic arithmetic, navigation, and the moral principles of the French constitution.

Article 3.

The teachers will be selected by the government commission.

Article 4.

They will be lodged at a national establishment with its own garden.

Article 5.

Their salary will be 1000 Francs in the cities and 800 Francs in the villages.

Article 6.

The salaries will be funded by the sale of the suppressed convents and monasteries.

Article 7.

The government commission will decide on where to locate the schools and how they will be administered.

BONAPARTE

Order

Head Quarters of Malta, 30 Prairial Year VI
(18th June, 1798)

Bonaparte, the general-in-chief issues the following order:

Article 1.

The bishop's authority concerns only ecclesiastic matters. All procedures concerning marriages will be administered by the civil and criminal justice department.

Article 2.

It is strictly forbidden for the bishop, ecclesiastics,

and the inhabitants of the island to receive any form of payment for administering the sacraments. Their duty is to administer them free of charge. Consequently, all current practices of making donations and such payments are abolished.

Article 3.
No foreign sovereign is allowed to exercise his influence on matters of religion or justice. Consequently no cleric, or inhabitant, has the right to resort to any papal or sovereign authority.

BONAPARTE

Order
Head Quarters of Malta, 30 Prairial Year VI
(18th June, 1798)

Bonaparte, the general-in-chief, issues the following order:

Article 1.
A yearly budget of up to 40,000 Francs will be set aside for the hospital from the sale of confiscated convents and monasteries and from existing allocations.

Article 2.
A sum of 300,000 Francs will be set aside from seized national property to settle the debts incurred by the

Grand Master.

Article 3.
We will sell 300,000 Francs worth of national property to fund the needs of the navy garrison.

Article 4.
We will sell 300,000 Francs worth of national property to fund the headquarters.

Article 5.
The government commissioner will work with the lands commissions to oversee the sale of these properties.

BONAPARTE

Order
Head Quarters of Malta, 30 Prairial Year VI
(18th June, 1798)

Bonaparte, the general-in-chief, issues the following order:

Article 1.
General Vaubois will deport the English and the Russian consuls to Rome within 48 hours.

Article 2.
If the two consuls are Maltese, the deportation will

last two years after which they will be allowed to return as long the French republic has no complaints about them.

BONAPARTE

Order
Head Quarters of Malta, 30 Prairial Year VI
(18th June, 1798)

Bonaparte, the general-in-chief, issues the following order:

Article 1.
The authorizing officer[1] will approve a credit of 3000 Francs per month, from the paymaster, for the artillery command:
- 4000 Francs per month for the combat engineers
- 25,000 Francs per month for the navy
- 3000 Francs per month for special needs granted to the commander-general

BONAPARTE

---

[1] Simon de Sucy (Correspondence de Napoleon)

To the Foreign Minister
Head Quarters of Malta, 30 Prairial Year VI
(18th June, 1798)

Citizen Minister, I am sending you the frigate *la Sensible*. In Malta you will obtain news of my arrival in the East. I delayed the departure of the frigate because I felt it was important that it brings to you news of the taking of Malta.

It is with pleasure that I declare to you the high esteem I have towards you.

The fleet is leaving the harbour and in one hour I will board the flagship.

BONAPARTE

From General Vaubois
to General Bonaparte
Head Quarters of Malta, 27 Messidor Year VI
(15th July 1798)

We are facing difficulties with provisions caused by the powers of Naples and Sicily. Sicily is requiring our ships to do quarantine for no reason. Our sailors are being badly treated. We have written to the viceroy of Sicily to try to re-establish free commerce.

The Maltese are appreciating our presence more and more but even though they seemed so grateful during the friendly celebrations of July 14th[1], they are

---

[1] Bastille Day

still not keen on acquiring national property. Those resources may remain useless to us for quite some time. I am angry that we cannot fulfil all your plans due to the lack of money. I will be even more upset if we face more delays with wages.

Regardless of all my efforts, my men are showing signs of impatience. They have without doubt been lacking provisions but we took care of things as quickly as possible.

Generally speaking, I dare say, I am well liked on the island and it pains me to see my brothers in arms reacting badly towards me even though I do my best to ease their discomfort. I cannot hide the fact that I prefer to work with one integral disciplined corps rather than a combination of several units. However, the situation could be much better if money was not lacking. If by misfortune we have to delay wages by ten days we would face problems with some soldiers, of that I am sure. We can last until *Fructidor*[1] after which we are going to need new funds.

The government commission and the municipalities are doing very well. These people are so amiable, full of goodness and kindness. I observe them very closely and I have no reason to suspect any plots.

Three known English frigates are always within sight. They are hindering considerably our ability to bring in provisions. We are certain that English

---

[1] Late August

corsairs are being armed at Messina. They intend to starve us and the Sicilians are doing their best to support them.

In general we all get on well with each other over here. We do however disagree with Regnaud[1] concerning one point. I believe he is wrong for he is the only one with such an opinion and if he persists it will become a matter of honour. The topic is important because it concerns the administration of the *università*. He wants to appoint, as its head, a person of whom much is said against. This is the administration responsible for the provisioning of our troops. The wealth of many individuals is in its hands. Its treasury is in deficit but it could easily return to credit. It is too important and could face serious upheavals if it does not have the trust of the people. But we will not let things boil over; I am hopeful everything will be just fine.

Regnaud is a competent person but he can be arrogant and somewhat vain. I will oppose him only in the interest of the general public. In spite of our differing opinions there is no discord between us. Once I am convinced that something is right I cannot give in even though I am criticized for being too good.

VAUBOIS

---

[1] Regnaud de Saint-Jean-d'Angely the government commissioner

From Citizen Ransijat[I] to General Bonaparte
Head Quarters of Malta, 29 Messidor Year VI
(17th July 1798)

I take the liberty to inform you that the commission you have created to organize the new government is progressing well and with great zeal. We are pressing ahead as quickly as possible driven by the will to respond to the trust you have shown in us. We are happy that Maltese population is very willing to adopt the new form of government particularly those in the city who are more forward-thinking than those in the villages. The city folk were more exposed to the frustrations of the Order's rule. They were delighted to see the back of the knights. They seem to be growing more attached to the French that have remained on the island. During the nice celebrations we held here on the 26 *Messidor*[II], which will be eloquently described to you by Regnaud, we witnessed a touching testimony of harmony between us and the Maltese such that we seemed to be one united nation.

Generally speaking, the Maltese are immersed in superstition and ignorance, more so than any other nation. Nevertheless, I am hoping that they

---

[I] Former knight, treasurer of the Order who became president of the government commission. He published his diary of the occupation in 1801 translated into English in a book entitled "Blockade 1798" (Malta University Press)

[II] Bastille Day

will be quicker to adopt and adhere to the French constitution given their gentleness and their sweet nature.

They are enchanted by the kindness of General Vaubois who is an outstanding man and most appropriately chosen for the task you have assigned him with.

His openness has won him everyone's affection especially the members of government commission who are delighted with him. He is always ready and most willing to do whatever he can to be helpful. Consequently, citizen general, we have you to thank for giving us such a worthy gentleman who can influence so positively the Maltese population into adopting the new laws. I hope you will be happy with Malta on your return because the Maltese will be able to appreciate, as they should, the inestimable benefits of the freedom that you have given them.

RANSIJAT

From Citizen Ganteaume to General Bonaparte
Alexandria, 29 Messidor Year VI
(18th August 1798)

I am sending you the report by means, of General Kléber, concerning the disastrous events suffered by our navy. Having been the only general present during the attack, I feel obliged to inform you of the latest details of this tragic event.

After the attack, Admiral Nelson offered to disembark the wounded and other French prisoners on condition that they remained prisoners of war. General Kléber accepted to receive them in Alexandria and we have been taking care of these prisoners since the 15th.

We have received 8000 wounded so far and 2600 men have been landed ashore. We now have a more accurate account of the losses we incurred during that cruelly fatal night[i].

Captain Trulet and Captain Dalbarde both badly wounded; Captain Emenau, Blanquet, Etienne and Gilet all wounded; Captain Thevenard and Petit-Thouars, killed.

L'Orient caught fire after a four-hour combat against two, possibly three or four, enemy ships. The admiral was killed as I previously reported and poor Casabianca perished in the fire after being badly wounded in the leg and in the arms.

The captain of the *Timoleon* was forced to

---

[i] Napoleon's fleet was decimated by Nelson at Abukir Bay on August 1st 1798

shipwreck and burn his own ship, after saving his crew, in order not to have his ship fall into enemy hands. The *William Tell*, le *Genereux*, *la Diane*, and *la Justice* were the only ships to escape. They joined our frigate division in Alexandria. This division, although lacking in provisions, is heading for Malta or Corfu.

The English fleet has been in Bequiers since the 15th. They are busy repairing their own ships and those captured from us. We have little information about their losses but we are certain that Admiral Nelson is badly wounded in the head. We are reliably informed that he has been permanently blinded. Two of his captains were killed and 300 men are not fit for combat...

GANTEAUME

To the French Consul in Tripoli
Head Quarters of Malta, 1 Fructidor Year VI
(18th August 1798)

Citizen Consul, after we took Malta we sailed for Alexandria. We defeated the mamluks, we took Cairo and occupied the whole of Egypt. For the moment, the English have superiority over us at sea after having destroyed our squadron. That is why I ask of you to send a messenger from Tripoli to Malta, Civita-Vecchia, or Cagliari, from where he can easily reach Toulon by means of a Turkish *galiot*.

I am sending you a copy of the letter[I] to be delivered. You will say that the army has been victorious on land and has established itself in Egypt without losses or sick men. You will say that I am fine and that they should take no notice of any malicious rumours that are being spread in France.

Send me a messenger from Tripoli with any news you have from France and send a letter to Malta with instructions to send me all the gazettes they have. It is important that you send me, at least once every ten days, a messenger who will travel by sea up to Derna[II] and from there he can cross the desert. I will reimburse you for all the expense incurred. I will not risk sending money across the desert but if you know of a merchant in Tripoli who needs 6000 Francs in Cairo you can have them and issue a bill of exchange on me. I assure you I will

---

[I] The letter was never found (Correspondence de Napoleon)
[II] Libya

157

pay generously for each messenger that brings me important news.

Let the Bey know that tomorrow we celebrate the feast of the Prophet with great pomp. The caravan for Tripoli is leaving tomorrow; I have given it my protection for which they were grateful. Ask the Bey to send as many provisions as possible to Malta, and send sheep to Alexandria. Ask him also to let his people know that the caravans are protected by us.

BONAPARTE

Order
Head Quarters of Cairo, 9 Fructidor Year VI
(26th August 1798)

The general-in-chief, issues the following order:

Article 1.
Monge, Berthollet and Poussielgue will meet with the army paymaster tomorrow morning at seven to remove the seals of the diamonds we found in Malta.

Article 2.
Citizen Poussielgue will take with him two local jewellers who will estimate the worth of these precious stones. They must not be told of the price that was estimated in Malta. The items will be divided into four categories:

- Items that are easy to auction, that can be purchased by army officers or by local inhabitants
- Items that can be converted into coins
- Items that can be offered as gifts to Turkish leaders
- Items that could be sent back to France

Article3.

An inventory will be made of the items in each category with the estimated worth.

Article4.

The army paymaster is authorized to convert to coins the items of the second category.

Article 5.

The treasury administration will establish the regulations for auctioning the items in the first category.

BONAPARTE

To Brigade-General Chanez
Head Quarters of Cairo, 11 Fructidor Year VI
(28th August 1798)

I received your letter of the 12 *Thermidor*. I am very pleased to hear that your situation in Malta is very satisfactory and that you have everything you require to keep this important conquest in the hands of the republic. Our situation here is very satisfactory we are masters of the whole country. I will send you several accounts of the events that took place.

BONAPARTE

To Citizen Regnaud de Saint-Jean-d'Angely
Head Quarters of Cairo, 25 Fructidor Year VI
(10th September 1798)

Messenger Lesimple has delivered to me your letters of the 14 *Thermidor* and 8 *Fructidor*. They are more or less the only letters I have received.

It gives me great pleasure to learn of the good conduct that you are maintaining in Malta and the services you are rendering to the republic in managing this important base.

Things are looking good over here. Our situation is improving each day. The richness of this country in wheat, rice, vegetables, cotton, and sugar is matched only by the barbarism of its inhabitants.

But we are already seeing a change in their ways. In three or four years' time everything will be radically different over here.

You have no doubt received the letters I wrote you concerning the military events that took place. Take every opportunity to send all the news you have about us to France by means of *speronaras*[1]. It only takes one report form a neutral source to quell the never-ending rumours that are so easily believed by the gullible imbeciles in the big city.

BONAPARTE

From General Vaubois to
Chevalier Fossetti in Alexandria
Head Quarters of Malta (11th December 1800)

Sir, the Maltese have much endured and for so long. Although they complain I foresee no danger. They are easily intimidated and for the time being they are patient, wary, submissive, and silent. They seem forsaken by their natural courage and their fear of danger and hardship. But it is in this state that they are to be most mistrusted and feared. This calm is like our Mediterranean sky. On a fine summer's day, without any warning, a storm instantly breaks out, the heavens become dark and the unsuspecting vessel is tossed about and engulfed.

---

[1] Small but fast Maltese/Sicilian passenger boats

We gave the Maltese their freedom; they were governed by their own magistrates, without our interference. We guided them like our own children, when unfortunately we received new orders from France. Convinced that we could treat them as a conquered nation, we established new laws. As a result the whole country rebelled in an instant. In two hours, every man was up in arms; we were besieged, our troops were cut off in every part in the island. We thought we were in perfect security. There was no trace of discontent. They then besieged the garrison of Valletta from all sides. We attempted several counter attacks – we had to combat enraged lions – no trace of their former docile character remained. It became impossible to govern the country. English and Portuguese ships soon arrived and blockaded us by sea. After being shut for two years in the city of Valletta and having only one day's provision left, the English Generals granted us an honourable capitulation and sent us to France. Our troops had to embark before the Maltese were allowed to enter the city as those infuriated people would have ignored the agreement we made with the English. The outcome would have been dreadful to all parties since the English had no means of controlling them with only two or three hundred men on the island.

***

HISTORICAL BOOKS ABOUT MALTA
BY JOE SCICLUNA

By Order of Napoleon
The Taking of Malta
*A Compilation of Napoleon's Order's
concerning the taking and the
adminstration of Malta.*

BLOCKADE
Malta 1798 – 1800
Bosredon de Ransijat
*An eyewitness account
of the French Occupation*

THE MALTA SOLDIER
A Historical Novel
Inspired by True Events

Availble also in French and German

SWORD-LILY
The Last Days of the Knights of Malta
1798
*A Historical Novel by August de
Kermainguy written in 1843*

MALTA SURRENDERED
The Doublet Memoirs
*An Eyewitness Account of Napoleon's
Invasion of Malta in 1798*

About the Author

Born and raised on the island of Malta, I have has spent most of his life in the southeast of France, in the town of Grenoble nestled in the Alps. I draws a sense of balance from the stark contrast between this mountainous region and the sun-baked Mediterranean island which I still call home. As I get older, the more passionate I am about the culture and the heritage of the Maltese islands. It is precisely this passion that motivated me to publish my first two books which were translations of eyewitness accounts of Napoleon's invasion and the subsequent occupation in 1798. Following on this same theme, I wrote **The Malta Soldier**, a historical novel set in the early 19th century during the first years of Malta's British rule.

Made in the USA
Las Vegas, NV
03 December 2021

35973948R00095